THE COMMUNITY COLLEGE IN THE TWENTY-FIRST CENTURY

A Systems Approach

Michael Scott Cain

University Press of America,® Inc.
Lanham • New York • Oxford

Copyright © 1999 by
University Press of America,® Inc.
4720 Boston Way
Lanham, Maryland 20706

12 Hid's Copse Rd.
Cumnor Hill, Oxford OX2 9JJ

All rights reserved
Printed in the United States of America
British Library Cataloging in Publication Information Available

Library of Congress Cataloging-in-Publication Data

Cain, Michael Scott.
The community college in the twenty-first century : a systems approach / Michael Scott Cain
p.   cm.
Includes bibliographical references and index.
1. Community colleges—United States. 2. Community colleges—United States—Administration. 3. System theory. I. Title.
LB2328.15.U6C33   1999   378.1'543—dc21   99—12586 CIP

ISBN 0-7618-1357-8 (cloth: alk. ppr.)

```
LB 2328.15 .U6 C33 1999
Cain, Michael Scott.
The community college in the
twenty-first century
```

∞™ The paper used in this publication meets the minimum requirements of American National Standard for Information Sciences—Permanence of Paper for Printed Library Materials, ANSI Z39.48—1984

R01918 80664

CHICAGO PUBLIC LIBRARY
SOCIAL SCIENCES AND HISTORY
400 S. STATE ST   60605

CHICAGO PUBLIC LIBRARY
SOCIAL SCIENCES AND HISTORY
400 S. STATE ST   60605

CHICAGO PUBLIC LIBRARY

FORM 19

For my children

Shannon, Gabriel,

Rebecca, and Dahlia

Contents

Preface

Chapter 1	**The Wal-Mart of Higher Education**	1
Chapter 2	**An Overview of Systems Theory**	9
Chapter 3	**Four Generations of Confusion**	27
Chapter 4	**The Faculty**	41
Chapter 5	**Adjunct Faculty**	55
Chapter 6	**The Students**	77
Chapter 7	**Governing the Community College**	93
Chapter 8	**The Community College in the Twenty-First Century**	113

Bibliography 143

Index 150

Preface

The community college is now at a crucial place in its history. So much growth has happened so quickly that the schools are no longer what they were when most of the current faculty members and administrators began working in them. Over the past three decades, the schools have changed in appearance, in their goals, their missions, their student bodies and in their approaches. Whether you approve or disapprove of the directions in which the changes have taken the community college, you cannot dispute the fact that they are radically different.

I've spent my entire teaching career in community colleges. Unlike many of my colleagues, I went into the two-year college by choice. From the moment I stepped onto a community college campus as a student, I knew I wanted to teach in one. Once, a few years ago, when a friend and I were talking about how we wound up teaching in a community college, we mentioned the sense of idealism that led us there. My friend summed up the changes that had taken place since we'd begun working with students on our campus when he said, "Teaching in a community college used to be a crusade. Now it's just a good job."

I didn't agree with that statement then and I still don't. The community college is more than a good job. In fact, teaching in them is still a crusade. The public two-year colleges do not simply educate or credentialize. They change lives for the better. They change them radically and they change them permanently and they change them inexpensively. There is no other institution in American education that can take a young man or woman with a truly dismal previous school record and no academic accomplishment at all and offer him or her a chance to overcome all of that history, to become a different and better person academically and personally. In no other American system can a person fulfill the basic American myth: to go from nothing to something by her own effort.

Ours is a peculiarly American institution, one that could not have flourished elsewhere to the extent that it has here. Its essential Americanism is rooted in the fact that the two-year college has always reflected the *spirit* of the nation. It grew out of the national belief in self-development. The particular myth that governs the two-year college is this: everyone who can benefit from the process has both a right and an obligation to become educated.

From the beginnings of this nation, when Jefferson warned of the dangers of an uneducated population and George Washington called for a national university, Americans have mythologized education. We have always seen the learning process in quasi-religious terms that relate to the mysteries that lie deep within our minds and souls. As such, education has been called the key to the moral, social and intellectual development of our people and, as a result, to the nation as a whole.

The community college is the place where that development takes place. Our universities, like the European schools they modeled themselves upon, have always carried with them notions of the importance of royalty and aristocracy. The two-year college, however, has no such notions; it subscribes to the idea that drives the lower, middle and working classes in America - the idea that all citizens deserve an opportunity to become educated.

Samuel Eliot Morison (1965) writes

> By 1850 there had been formulated and to some extent established the basic principles of American education: (1) that free primary and secondary schools be available to all children: (2) that teachers should be given professional education, and (3) that all children be required to attend school to a certain age.... (532)

From 1850 until the present, the dominant story in American education has been the growth of those three principles. As a response to the direction in which the nation developed, the principles were extended both horizontally to other segments of our population, such as minorities and women, and vertically to include college and graduate schools.

That growth resulted in the development of the community college. As the horizontal extension of Morison's principles created wider access to primary and secondary schools, more of our citizens graduated from them and demanded access to post-secondary education. The states responded by enlarging the educational pie. In the nineteenth century, they responded by creating of the land-grant colleges.

The twentieth century saw the creation of the public two-year college. The community college is to the twentieth century, then, what the land grant college was to the nineteenth. It is the place where the promise is kept. All of the underpinnings of the American myth of self-development and access to education are found in the basic beliefs of the community college. They were founded to provide wider opportunity to all people, including those whose previous histories demonstrated that up until this point, at least, they have not been able to take advantage of that opportunity.

The essential optimism of the two-year college is reflected in the fact that most will even grant chances to the functionally illiterate, believing that the students will develop their reading and writing skills to the point where they can benefit from higher education. "Even if they fail," one reading teacher told me, "they've gotten something out of being here. Next time, they might make it."

The dualistic nature of the community college. We must recognize that an odd duality which has always been buried deeply in the American psyche affects the community college. Like some not fully understood Buddhistic concept, the precise opposites of all of the major ideas we live by are found within us. We believe in progress, for example, but we are deeply conservative. A man should rise but he should not get beyond his neighbors; as we used to say in the south, you don't want to grow beyond your raising. Others contradictions abound. We should better ourselves economically while remembering that money is the root of all evil. We should shun gambling while buying state-sponsored lottery tickets. We retreat as we march forward, snatch away as we give, place limitations on power even as we bestow it. An advance in any area, such as feminism or civil rights, always brings on a backlash.

This progressive-conservative split is evident in education. Our schools exist to permit people to create a better future, but they see their role as passing on the culture of the past. They look forward with their eyes resolutely focused backwards. Even American upward mobility contains a two-valued schism. We worship the masses but desire to become members of an elite. At the same time, though, we distrust the elite. Only in this country do people take pride in describing themselves as average.

The duality of American thinking has greatly affected the community college. Consider our distrust of outside control. We insist on being in control of our own destiny; the nation marches on but the march must be led by thousands of individual neighborhoods. The community college is intended to affect the national destiny, but it must operate under local control.

Consider also our national tendency to place faith in action rather then theory, our insistence that a strong pragmatic element be present in whatever we put our faith in. Only Americans say "to see it is to believe it." Other nations trust abstractions.

Even as we study at institutions of higher learning, we deplore ivory tower intellectualism. Thinking is regarded as a virtue only if it leads to action. The learned man who is a figure of ridicule because he cannot do anything "practical" is a familiar American stereotype. Ichabod Crane, remember, was a teacher. Americans have a way of valuing knowledge while distrusting ideas.

These dualisms have always existed within the community college. The school tries to improve the life of Americans while strongly distrusting any hint of the elitism that might result from the improvement. It tries to develop people intellectually while being resolutely anti-intellectual itself and it tries to resist its own symbology.

This book is written out of a love of the community college. As I said, I chose to teach in one and have always been rewarded by that choice. I've seen students who have been written off as hopeless suddenly come alive intellectually and succeed. I've seen people become startlingly aware of their own power to achieve their goals and desires. I've seen people turn their lives around. Yesterday, for example, I received a letter from a former student telling me I would be meeting her sister when the fall semester began. "The good news," my student wrote, "is that she passed all of her courses - with C's and B's mostly. The bad news is that she missed fifty-five days of school and has been told by her high school that she can't come back." My student, who came alive as a student during her community college years, advised her sister to enter immediately. The sister will probably do well. I've encountered students like her many times over the years and they generally do.

In fact, I've been a part of these transformations often enough to know that they are not only possible but that they are actually everyday occurrences. On these campuses, the American dream can become a reality.

Perhaps because I know what is possible, I, like everyone else who works in the two-year college system, become frustrated by what is actually achieved most of the time and by the institution's loss of direction and loss of belief in itself. This book traces those problems and tries to suggest how they can be changed. The thesis of the book is that the problems the colleges face were inherent from the beginnings and became more prominent because the particular vantage points from which the schools were viewed prohibited the taking of any action on the problems.

Chapter one presents a portrait of what the colleges have become, establishing the governing metaphor of the book: the community college as the Wal-Mart of higher education. It argues that in the true spirit of American dualism, being the Wal-Mart of higher education is at one and the same time a good and a bad thing. Whether we see the good or the bad, however, we have to recognize that it is a choice that we made.

Chapter two presents the basic idea that this monograph uses to govern the examination of the community college, systems theory. This chapter argues that no institution can be fully understood by subjecting it to a specialist-oriented, linear examination. Institutions are actually systems and to be fully understood, need to be looked at from a systems perspective. The chapter gives the basics of system theory as it applies to the two-year college.

In chapter three, the conditions and events that led to the unchecked growth of the community college are examined. The unifying idea is that our present problems grew out of the fact that no one was at the wheel when the system grew into the sprawling mess that it is. It reacted to various stimuli instead of acting so that now, almost a full century into its development, no one can say with certainty exactly what the community college is. Depending on who is speaking for it, it claims to be all things to all people and that is a prime source of its current confusion.

The discussion then turns to the important elements of the system. Chapter four discusses the academic and vocational-technical faculty, showing that a split has always been present between them and that, in truth, neither of them works in exactly the same school. The central result of this split has been a loss of personal and professional power for both.

Chapter five concentrates on part-time faculty, which on some campuses, outnumbers full-time. These gypsy teachers face problems of their own, standing apart from other faculty members and the college as a whole. If full-time faculty members have lost power over the institution's history, the situation for adjuncts has been even worse; part-timers have never had any power. Over-reliance on them threatens the very fabric of the college.

Chapter six examines the reason we're all here, the students. Its central idea is that two-fold. Systemically, students have a much greater impact on the schools than we have previously imagined; they are not simply consumers. They are also much a more varied and complex lot than most discussions have suggested. So varied are they, in fact, that no generalization about them is fully true.

Chapter seven looks at the administration of the schools. Its essential notion is that governance of the community college constitutes a crisis and that few of the ideas suggested are likely to solve that crisis. In all of its history, the two-year college has never established a form of governance that is its own. It has borrowed from universities, from corporations and businesses, and has always assumed that those models would work when experience shows clearly that they have not and will not. A major factor in the crisis in governance is that administrations are not aware of the systemic properties of the institutions they attempt to run and therefore try to manage them instead of leading them.

Finally, chapter eight attempts to put on the table a few ideas that will help us move toward solutions. It does not provide a complete model for the community college - such a model is beyond the scope of this book - but it does try to identify a few of the qualities that such a model would have. A total model is out of the question because of the local control under which colleges operate and because of the fact that each school is a unique entity in itself. Trying to standardize a highly individual institution is one of the mistakes that led us into this situation. The goal of the chapter is modest: it intends to start a dialogue which will lead to appropriate solutions for each campus.

This, then, is a book that criticizes the community college as it now exists. Let me emphasize that it does so lovingly. As a part of the system, I am partially responsible for the problems as well as the successes, so I can only criticize with optimism, hope and love. Although this book is not technically a research study, it is based on both library and field research. The research comes from sources but all of the inferences drawn from the research are mine. The original authors should not be blamed for any misinterpretations or faulty conclusions I have derived from their work.

During the years this book was in preparation, literally hundreds of people spoke to me, formally or informally, about the issues discussed in it. There are far to many to name, so I wish to offer a group thank you and give my appreciation to all who contributed. You know who you are.

Chapter 1:

The Walmart of Higher Education?

Although community colleges have had the largest impact of any institution of higher education in this century, they remain misunderstood. The literature is rich with both descriptions and prescriptions; each interested party has his own view of exacty what the institution is and what it should be. Each loudly declares what direction the colleges should take in the future. Looking at a community college is like looking in a slightly askew mirror; the viewer sees a reflection of his own needs, desires and ideology.

Proponents of vocational education see them as extensions of high school trades programs, while those who advocate four-year degree programs emphasize the transfer function. Some, as Dale Parnell does in his influential book, *The Neglected Majority*, try to walk a tight line between career prep and transfer. Most of the tight-walkers, however, wind up, as Parnell does, in the career prep camp. Still other researchers see the community college as the land of the last chance, offering the educationally disenfranchised one more opportunity to pick up essential learning skills so that college becomes a genuine option. Others see the job of the community college as a salvage operation. Those who hold this view see the purpose of the college as salvaging not simply students but entire communities, a sort of institution-as-social-worker philosophy.

Opinions are not confined to educators. Politicians, both local and national, periodically decide that the community college is an appropriate place to develop whatever skills, techniques or occupations they consider important to the future of either the region or the country.

With so many competing views, it is difficult to nail down precisely what the institution truly is. As we shall see, nothing about the community college is easily defined or described. As the new educational plans and programs float out of the political arena, such as President Clinton's 1997 call for two years of college for each of the nation's high school graduates, it will be more important to make sense out of that amorphous animal, the community college.

One thing is certain: The community college resists easy definition because it is something brand new in American education. Almost without recognizing what we were doing, we created a truly unique institution, one that follows no pre-existing models.

The fact that the community college has no previous models makes it difficult to get a handle on just what it is and what it ought to be; it is too many things at once. Although some will not find the metaphor flattering, the community college has become the Wal-Mart of American education. Conveniently located, with lots of parking, offering something for everyone, maintaining good quality at low prices, with hours that allow for flexible shopping, and a commitment to personal service, the community college, like the discount chain, seeks to make itself indispensable to the neighborhood.

Let us explore the Wal-Mart metaphor in some detail:

The image. Wal-Mart's goal is not simply to serve shoppers. It aims to create an awareness in the public mind; when a need surfaces, Wal-Mart's management wants the public to believe that their stores are the natural place to satisfy it. It has succeeded in its reeducation campaign to such an extent that it is now more than simply one of many places to shop. The chain has become a major force in American life. For reasons similar to the ones that allowed Wal-Mart to become the dominant presence that it is, the community college has also become a major force in American life.

Convenient location. Community colleges go where the people are. Since they are generally non-resident commuter colleges, they are placed in high population density areas, where their clients can reach them without difficulty. Since they usually operate under local, rather than state, control, they are located in high profile areas of the cities or counties they serve.

In the event that their primary campuses are not convenient, most community colleges also offer off-campus branches, ranging from full scale duplications of the main campus in other locations to single class offerings in senior centers, businesses and corporations, storefronts, community centers and other schools. If you wish to study at a university, you travel to it. A community college comes to you.

Like Wal-Mart, the community college takes the idea of access seriously.

Something for everyone. The Wal-Mart chain achieved its retail prominence by promoting the idea of one-stop shopping. Because of the range of retail offerings, it is no longer necessary to visit several specialty stores.

The community college extends the one-stop shopping idea to education. Under one roof, you can find academic transfer programs, vocational training, terminal semiprofessional programs such as those for mechanics and morticians, non-credit enrichment courses, one-shot seminars, televised courses, and interactive video seminars. If a need exists, a community college administrator somewhere in this country is searching for a way to meet it. Should the need not exist, that same administrator may see it as his duty to create it. Since many of the offerings are funded by grants, some administrators have created programs in order to qualify for grant funding, even when the program was not essential to the area they serve. Instead of reacting to a real need, these presidents and deans have tried to anticipate one by creating the program and then creating a need for it through the use of promotion techniques not so very different from the ones used to sell detergent at Wal-Mart, such as radio and TV ads.

These institutions truly see it as their duty to offer something for everyone. The idea that a segment of the population is not being both personally and professionally developed as a result of their work is anathema. As one president said:

> Our colleges help move people from lesser to greater states: from unformed ambitions to clear career goals; from immigrant status to competent citizen; from financial dependence to economic independence; from high school graduate to third year university student; from the unskilled to the fully licensed; from the confused to the informed. (Rouche, Baker and Rose, 1989, p. 130)

Truly, something for everyone.

One area in which both the critics and the proponents of community colleges are in agreement is that overall the quality is sound. Students who wish to succeed are able to do so. Most students who transfer do well at the schools they move on to; indeed, long range tracking studies show that even a surprisingly high percentage of "terminal" students proceed over time to become transfer students. In urban areas, up to ninety percent of graduates of terminal technical or vocational programs enter an upper division academic program within five years of concluding their terminal courses. Successful community college students are generally able to take advantage of their future opportunities.

Good quality, low prices, convenient hours. Students confuse the studies even more by taking advantage of the flexibility of the schools. Critics point to high drop-out rates as an indication of failure; after all, most community colleges lose about forty percent of their students. Four out of every ten students who enter a community college leave the school without finishing. As proponents of the schools insist, however, these figures are elusive, difficult to interpret. Most of the students who make up that forty percent are not actually lost. They do not drop out; instead they "stop out," taking time off and then returning. Most community college students take an average of five years to complete a two-year course of study.

So, what critics see as a failure is actually an indicator of the flexibility of the institution, a clear response to a community need for a model that will permit non-traditional students to succeed.

The use of drop-out figures as a measure of failure also indicates that the nature of the institution is not understood. Community colleges are measured by a sort of double standard; when a university has a forty percent drop-out rate among its freshmen and sophomores, the number is viewed as a sign of high quality and rigorous standards. Should a community college have that same statistic, it is viewed as a failure.

Because they are different entities, traditional four year colleges and universities naturally operate by a different set of rules. Like sales reps for expensive, exclusive products, the upper division schools pre-qualify their students, accepting only those who are likely to experience success. Like Wal-Mart, community colleges do not pre-qualify. Their role is to serve the disenfranchised. The community college views itself as an open-door institution, serving whoever shows up at the gates.

This insistence on the open door has been its strength and its weakness; it offers another chance to those who do not succeed quickly and, its critics say, it cynically offers dozens of chances to people who will never be able to take advantage of them. As long as bodies are in the seats and tuition is in the till, the critics say, the colleges consider things to be just fine.

In its efforts to throw wide the doors, to democratize education and to provide a wide-ranging set of academic instructional programs for everyone, the community college encounters problems that other institutions are able to dance around. Few universities, for example, attempt to provide training in basic literacy. Nearly every community college does so routinely. Few universities see it as their duty to take an ill-equipped, math-phobic, grammatically-warped, GED-carrying kid off of the streets from scratch to move on to the status of college graduate. Most community colleges do so as a matter of course; indeed, they consider doing so a part of their mission.

The fact of the matter is everyone who deals with them, from administrators to counselors to faculty members, realize that a lot of those ill-equipped people are not going to achieve their desires and that critics are going to hold the community college responsible for their failures. Advocates consider this assignment of blame unfair. Because many of its students show up without academic preparation, the community college must provide devel-opmental instruction. Every developmental program at every institution suffers huge levels of attrition; that is the reality and that reality does not indicate the failure of the community college as much as it does the failure of American public education as a whole. To blame the community college for that failure is like placing the blame for AIDS on a lack of morality in the public at large: convenient, certainly, and, if you stretch it to its limits, possibly containing a partial grain of accuracy, but hardly true.

Because of its open-door policy, its relatively low cost and its mission to offer services to the entire community, the community college faces problems unique to itself. It maintains a high degree of quality despite those problems.

Personal service. Just like Wal-Mart, the community college does everything it can to make partaking of its offerings an easy task. Few other institutions permit a person to make a decision to attend the school, fill out the application, register and go to the classes she has chosen the same day. The colleges aim for a degree of personal service and flexibility that allow the maximum number of students to shop.

Just as the sales help makes selecting from a staggering choice of items a simpler task, the community college's advisement and counseling personnel offer guidance on a first-come, first served basis. Just as the credit department helps people buy, the schools work to make loans, scholarships and work-study programs available to the financially impaired. And just as the credit department works with a customer who stretches himself too thin, the centers provide backup and support services for students who find themselves in academic trouble.

Community colleges pride themselves on valuing their clients both as students and as people. Just as Wal-Mart aims to be friendly to their customers, the schools work at being close to their clientele. Indeed, the operational phrase is "student-centered" and, from the beginning, this attitude has been identified as one of the most important attributes of these schools. Students, faculty and administrators all identify this student-centered closeness as a major strength of the schools, an important factor in student success.

Wal-Mart knows that many shopping options exist - everything from Macy's to Saks Fifth Avenue to K-Mart is available at the mall - and that its continued success must come from its personal relationship to its customers. The community colleges have internalized this same lesson.

Pragmatism. As I said in the beginning, many people will find the Wal-Mart metaphor distasteful. Although Wal-Mart is an increasingly important part of the American retail landscape, it is not perceived the same way Abercromby and Fitch, Nordstrom or Bloomingdale's are; shopping there does not confer status. Even the chain's most loyal customers do not point with pride to the fact that they furnished parts of their homes with its products.

No, they go there for purely pragmatic reasons, not symbolic ones, and that is another common denominator the retail chain shares with the community college. The majority of the two-year college's students attend because academic, financial or life conditions make it impossible for them to be elsewhere; they must be practical about their education.

Like Wal-Mart, the community college is an institution of the masses, not the elite. The notion of service to the masses is a peculiarly American one and is responsible for shaping the community college into the force it has become.

Discussion. Although Wal-Mart is a metaphor that eliminates any idea of elitism, it is still not an entirely bad thing for an institution of higher learning to resemble the retail chain. The store-school correlation offers a mixed bag of strengths and weaknesses.

The prime strengths of the community colleges are their openness and flexibility. The colleges provide an option for those who feel their options are closed off. When a woman in her late thirties, with a dozen years in a job she enjoys in a firm in which she intends to build a career, discovers she can only reach the next level of success by acquiring the degree she did not feel qualified to pursue when she was eighteen, where does she go? When another woman in her late twenties recognizes that life in a touring rock band is no way to raise two young daughters and determines that she needs more education, what are her options? The community college is the only place for these people, whom we will meet in a later chapter, to go.

Increasing the options has increased the availability of higher education and, indeed, this has been the single greatest strength of the community college. As far back as 1931, Walter Crosby Eells, then editor of *Junior College Journal*, speculated whether education beyond high school was to be the privilege of the classes or the boon of the masses:

> Going to college has become the great American habit. The junior college should be the "people's college" and available to all. It should provide collegiate opportunity for the mass of high school graduates who can't, won't, or shouldn't be university students. (192)

Eells coined the phrase "the democratization of higher education" to describe the institution's ability to provide higher education to those for whom it was not previously available.

A major strength of the community college, then, has been its ability to discover and serve what Wal-Mart would call new markets.

Ironically, its major weakness emanates from that same ability. The need to grow and spread like a garden weed has caused what we might call the "Something for Everyone Syndrome," which was first described by Robert Hutchins:

> It [the community college] is confused, confusing, and contradictory. It has something for everybody. It is generous, ignoble, bold, timid, naive and optimistic. It is filled with the spirit of universal brotherhood and the sense of American superiority. It has great faith in money. It has great faith in courses. It is antihumanistic and antiintellectual. It is confident its vices can be turned into virtues by making them larger. Its heart is in the right place; its head does not work very well. (Quoted in O'Connell, 1968, 7-8)

Hutchins made that statement in 1954, during the first flush days of the junior college movement. Imagine what he'd say about the comprehensive community college which has emerged since those days.

Assumptions. In our rush to become Wal-Mart, we make assumptions that would make Hutchins spin: we assume that a functionally illiterate person can take credit level college courses while learning to read. We assume that ability does not matter; interest is the standard. We assume that an open door is a revolving door.

In the name of student-centeredness we assume that the students' success or failure is not their responsibility but ours:

> There are times when it really bothered me that students just all of a sudden disappeared. You work for six weeks or a semester; you're bringing them along;

you are exerting a lot of, you know, cheerleading energy and a lot of your professional energy as well; you're conjuring up all kinds of ways to help this guy and he's making some progress; it's slow, it's painful, but he is doing it. And then all of a sudden bang, you know, ... he's not in class.... The suspicion is gnawing that I didn't do enough.... (Seidman, 1984)

Just as Wal-Mart feels that it is their fault if a customer does not buy, the community college faculty and administration believe themselves to be at fault if everyone does not take advantage of their offerings.

And just as a growing number of people are returning to the strip shops because Wal-Mart has gotten too big and noisy and confusing, so are a number of people expressing dissatisfaction with the community college because it has overextended itself. It has lost its direction by spreading itself too thin. By trying to appeal to the entire population, it has wound up satisfying no one.

During its glory days, Wal-Mart grew by satisfying a pre-existing demand. Today, it tries to continue growth by creating that demand. A generation or so ago, in 1964, the social critic Paul Goodman pointed out that when an economy turned from satisfying a demand to attempting to create one, it was forced to rely on artificial rather than organic growth, a situation which was fraught with danger and could be seen as a sign of the decline of that economy.

The community college might be entering that phase. No organization can be all things to all people. Without a fresh sense of direction to unify its growth and efforts, the system we have created will alter beyond our recognition. As we go into the last decade of this century, as the community college enters a new generation of its history, instead of Wal-Mart, it might become one of those lesser chains, dingy in decline, offering nothing of value, and inexorably creeping toward bankruptcy.

This book is about that possibility. Its intention is to help the two-year colleges avoid becoming the educational equivalent of, say, the Ames chain. To accomplish this goal, the book will examine the current state of the community college, determine how it got into that state, and offer suggestions on a direction to take. If this new sense of forward motion in a different direction can be accomplished, then the community college can become the major educational force of the twenty-first century. It deserves to have that title and that function. This book intends to help it acquire them.

Chapter 2:

An Overview of Systems Theory

Perhaps because, like Wal-Mart, the community college is ubiquitous, it remains misunderstood. Some critics charge that the schools have grown like weeds in the nation's educational garden, springing up unchecked, spreading randomly. Also like unchecked weeds, the community college is everywhere. It has grown without fanfare to become the dominant force in undergraduate higher education; along with its flexibility, its Wal-Mart qualities insure that, if it continues to truly serve its public, the institution's dominance will increase.

For all that, though, we do not understand the community college. Because we do not truly understand it, the school has, like some its students, never become all that it could be; it has never maximized its potential. One reason it has remained promising rather than accomplished is because it has insisted on continually re-inventing itself. Despite the fact that the first junior college was started in 1915 and that the comprehensive community college emerged in the early sixties, we who operate the system are still arguing loudly and angrily about what the community college should be.

To be still debating that question this late in its history indicates that the community college has not imprinted itself in the academic mind as an established entity. As far back as 1960, the pressures of adaptation caused the then current state of the community college to be described as "ambiguous, while weakening the ability of administrators to maintain and defend goals." (Quoted in Palinchak, 1973) The descent of the schools into confusion and ambiguity was described long before the two-year school morphed into the current model, the comprehensive community college. That shift intensified the institution's problems by increasing the ambiguity. It became exponentially more difficult in maintain the community college's goals. Defending the institution and those goals to critics of the schools became even more difficult.

To understand why the community college is still in search of its identity, we must start from the premise that it is, in fact, a unique institution whose overall place in the structure of American education has *never* been made completely clear. The fact is that, although its origins may have been in other institutions, over the past four decades, the community college has evolved into a system entirely its own. Like Wal-Mart, the institution might be similar to others, but the resemblances are superficial; a deeper look reveals originality. In actuality the community college is something brand new in education and can only be understood by an examination that takes a new approach. This book provides that approach. Rather than falling back on the linear and singular approach that usually guides discussions such as this one, this book examines the institution from a systems perspective.

To make this perspective clear, a brief overview of systems theory is necessary.

The age of the specialist. The knowledge explosion has created such a huge amount of information that no single individual can keep up with it. Due to the explosion, becoming an expert in any given field is a goal that has been rendered quite unachievable - instead, researchers seek to become experts in a *part* of a field, an area of specialization. It is safe to say that we live in the age of the specialist.

Specialization has led to tremendous increases in knowledge but in many fields, higher education among them, it has also led to a shrinking of focus, a type of scholarly tunnel-vision that prevents us from understanding the whole. It is as though we view the world through binoculars held backwards and assume that what we see is all that exists. We have achieved an accurate and detailed look at the parts but cannot assemble them into a total package. Like a mother trying to put together her child's bicycle on Christmas Eve, we have trouble conceptualizing how this collection of parts can add up to a total package that is simultaneously a toy, a means of transportation, an exercise machine, a source of pride and joy, and an object of symbolic importance.

Specialization has not led, however, to an increase in the communication of knowledge. In fact, the opposite has occurred. As fields grow more arcane and exotic, scholars can communicate with each other when their specialties match, but will almost invariably experience difficulty when they step outside their chosen area. This is true not only in both the hard and soft sciences but within the liberal arts as well. A scholar of archetypal theory in beat literature who meets a specialist in Germanic ethics in Old English poetry often finds that, although both of them are professors of English, they have no common basis for communication. They resort to discussing academic politics, a field in which they both have a general knowledge.

Specialization, then, divides. Rather than leading to a fuller understanding of the whole, it is like viewing the image on a movie screen: sharp and detailed in the area brought to the foreground, but soft and fuzzy everywhere else. Specialization examines carefully isolated phenomena. In the examination, other phenomena which contribute to the totality are lost. In the field of psychology, for instance, for most of this century, behavioral specialists declared that consciousness did not exist because it could not be observed or measured. Consciousness researchers rejected behaviorism just as strongly.

Since, in order to achieve the total picture, a synthesis of both of these fields (and a lot more) is essential, the whole suffered. Specialization is not to be rejected out of hand. It has made a partial and segmented understanding of a great many things possible. It should be understood, however, that specialization leads only to partial knowledge. The whole remains elusive. It is the difference between *a* truth and *the* truth.

The need for a new focus. The truth is obscured, buried in myth, legend, and judgment, and therefore hard to locate. It is the whole, not the individual parts and most specialists cannot explain that elusive whole. A crowd, for example, is more than a gathering of a sum of individuals. It is not counted heads. Numerous social scientists have pointed out that a crowd takes on a personality of its own that is not the totality of the personalities of the individuals that make it up. To study the individuals does not lead to insights about the nature of the crowd. To gain insights about the crowd, the whole, a new focus is needed.

To take an example from popular culture, the Nitty Gritty Dirt Band has been a noted country-rock group for more than three decades. During that time, more than thirty different musicians have been members of the group. It has sometimes been a sextet, sometimes a quintet and sometimes a quartet, yet the sound, attitude and musical approach of the band has remained the same for more than thirty years. The Dirt Band has maintained a collective identity that is more than and different from the identity of its members. The band, then, can best be described and understood as a system.

Similarly, Wal-Mart has been spreading across the nation as quickly and completely as community colleges. Sam Walton, the founder of the chain, died in the early eighties. A new set of executives manage the company now. Yet no matter which individuals make up the management and staff of the firm at any given time, the "personality" of the company remains the same.

The Nitty Gritty Dirt Band and Wal-Mart are examples of systems - holistic totalities that convey meaning. To understand that conveyed meaning, it is essential to study the system, not its parts. Specialists study separate aspects of the total, parts of it. They pick and choose, a touch of this and a smidgen of that, as though they had suddenly found themselves attending some kind of research buffet.

What is important, however, is the whole. Meaning does not come from the individual components of a thing, but from the way these components interact to produce the totality. Specialists cannot study the interaction that produces the whole.

Systems theorists can.

Systems theory. Even as the age of the specialist flourished, many of the discoveries that it offered up as its contributions undermined it. As the scientific method became the dominant paradigm, it insisted that theories which could not be empirically measured or tested be discarded. As a result, theology, philosophy and the philosophically-oriented psychologies, such as the Humanistic approaches, suffered.

By explaining much of life and casting off that which could not be explained, science brought forth the concept of the mechanistic age, in which all of the work of the world, everything from thought to action to feeling, was thought to be some sort of giant machine. Today, the metaphor has shifted; we describe the workings of the natural world as resembling a giant computer and construct elaborate models designed to show its operation - but the metaphor, even though we recognize its inadequacies, remains essentially the same, as mechanistic as a steam boat.

Knowledge continually outruns our attempts to understand it. As hard as we strive for clarity, the unexplained hovers as though it were an old song we can't get out of our minds. Even as the more conservative scientific approaches created the models, frontier sciences were destroying them. In physics, new knowledge attained by the prevailing mechanical model undercut the mechanistic model so completely that Relativity and Quantum Theory soon took over. Similar revolutions in other sciences followed.

The mechanistic model was continually forced to face the fact that a collection of empirically proven facts did not add up to a picture of the totality. A box of matches is not a fire. It became increasingly evident that something was missing.

Systems theory evolved as an effort to search for that missing thing.

Systems theory is generalist as opposed to specialist. It examines the totality, not its parts. The totality, the complete entity, rather than being a collection of individual pieces, is a system - a specific structure made up of certain maintained relationships among its parts. The system is the *whole*, not just the parts but the way they interact with each other. As the pieces relate, they create a whole that transcends the number of parts. Meaning, significance and both literal and symbolic importance come from the interactions of parts, not the parts themselves.

Systems theory, then, examines the regularities or redundant patterns we observe between people and other phenomena. What this means is that any given pattern of relationships is described as a system.

Every system, whether it be a family, a giant retail chain, a school or a rock band, manifests irreducible characteristics of its own. As stated, each member of a band has an individual identity. The band itself, however, is a system with its own identity which rises from the relationships between the individual members. The system will maintain itself for as long as it exhibits certain precise characteristics of its own. Meaning comes from the interactive relationships between those characteristics.

To gain meaning, then, it is necessary to examine the system.

The characteristics of systems. How can systems be understood? Laszlo (1972) says that natural systems have four invariable characteristics:

1: They are wholes with irreducible properties.
We have seen that the whole, like Wal-Mart, the Dirt Band or a family, is more than the sum of its parts. As we have noted, parts can be replaced with others. An executive may retire or resign to join one of the competitors but since the system is a whole, it does not disappear or radically alter when these changes take place.

In a school, students, faculty and administrators come and go, but the school remains the same. Each individual member of the system fits into its slot and exerts its influence on the other members.

The mysterious element that makes the system a whole, its personality or identity, comes from the totality. Each member contributes but all of the contributions in some way combust to become something more than the sum of the parts. Systems are not simply a collection of people; they consist of people plus *their relationships*. As Laszlo writes

> The most basic unit consists of two parts in communication, where the outcome is something more than the simple sum of the properties of their relationship.... If this is doubted by the skeptical reader, let him consider Plato's great discovery: the dialectic. According to Plato, two people, by challenging and responding to each other can get closer to the truth than either one could by himself. (p. 28-29)

2: Systems maintain themselves in a changing environment.

Although systems can have many goals, the dominant one is always survival. Like a bureaucracy (a system in itself) the system seeks to perpetuate itself. To understand how this principle operates, consider an example once used by John Steinbeck. In *The Log From the Sea of Cortez* (1951), he described how, while watching a school of fish, he was struck by a complete certainty that humans have fundamentally misunderstood the operation of the school. We have always assumed that each fish was primary when, in reality, the school was the primary organism and each individual fish, though it had its own little life, was more importantly a part of the life of the larger animal, the school. Each individual fish was to the school what a cell is to the human body:

> There must be some fallacy in thinking of these fish as individuals.... Their functions in the school are in some as yet unknown way as controlled as though the school was one unit. We cannot think of this intricacy until we are able to think of the school as an animal in itself, reacting with all its cells to stimuli which perhaps might not influence one fish at all.
> And this larger animal, the school, seems to have a nature and drives and ends of its own. It is more than and different from the sum of its parts. (p. 240)

The fish school Steinbeck has described is an example of a system. As is the case with all systems, the purpose of the school was to survive and the survival of the total organism was more important than the survival of any single cell. To Steinbeck, that survival-centered consciousness explained why the school was able to function as a single unit. He had wondered, as we all have, how hundreds of individual animals are able to swim in such a tight formation, executing exactly the same maneuvers at the same time. The answer he arrived at is summed up in the quote above. The school was able to behave with such choreographed precision because all of its members were in some fundamental and important way the same animal, each a single intelligence which contributed to and created the group intelligence. Exactly how a collection of individual intelligences can create a group intelligence remains poorly understood. It does, however, happen.

Steinbeck's speculation was, of course, a description of systems theory and his important contribution was the notion of the primary importance of the survival of the group as a goal. Each system is designed to seek self-maintenance, the way a human body seeks homeostasis, the condition where temperature, blood pressure, body chemicals and the rest hold steadily at a level that allows us to continue life.

The drive for homeostasis explains the seeming rigidity of systems. Since it is designed for self-maintenance and homeostasis, change comes slowly to a system; it results from gradual evolution rather than sudden shock.

3: Systems create themselves in response to the challenge of the environment.

If a system could only maintain itself, it would eventually undergo entropy and die. Systems, however, generate a creative force within them that permits them to alter as circumstances require, to answer stimuli not simply with conditioned responses but to create new responses.

Self-maintenance is a complex process; the system desires stability, but stability will inevitably lead to entropy, which, of course, will destroy the system. To maintain health, it must be able to change. Yet change also threatens the system. Therefore, survival demands a gradual, system-enhancing type of growth. Speer (1970) called this type of growth *morphogenesis*, a type of system-healthy behavior that allows for innovation, change and creativity. Healthy systems demand these factors because their presence promotes morphogenetic, ie., evolutionary, growth, rather than sudden revolutionary alteration. The system is not threatened but is still able to respond to the various challenges supplied by the environment.

Morphogenesis results from the natural push each element in the system generates as a series of actions and reactions. A recalcitrant administration, for example, tends to create a revolutionary faculty. Similarly, a faculty that demands rapid large scale change creates a resistant administration. Morphogenesis, therefore, permits change which takes place within the established rules of the system. When presented with the possibility of radical change which violates the established rules, systems promote stability, ie, *morphostasis*.

4: Natural systems are coordinating interfaces in nature's hierarchy.

Systems associate integrally with other systems. A pattern of mutual dependency exists. Each person belongs to many systems - family, school, business, church - and none can exist without the others. Corporate systems, for example, depend on school systems to educate potential employees and customers.

All aspects of life, then, constitute an interconnected chain of systems, just as nature itself is an ecological chain. Steinbeck's school of fish belongs to a chain of being in which each individual life supports all life. The system that the school of fish represents is an integral part of other systems, both larger and smaller, that creates a food chain that eventually supports our own lives.

Systems, then, rely on other systems for sustenance, maintenance and growth.

Discussion. By studying the system instead of a specialized part of it, we can better understand the totality. By subjecting the community college to a systemic examination, we can begin to understand why the confusion exists about its role. The remainder of this chapter will indicate some directions the examination will take.

The structure of the examination will follow the four characteristics of systems:

A system is a whole with irreducible properties. Viewed traditionally, the administration and faculty are in place to serve a student body. In theory, each September, students show up and choose from the offerings. They march through the curriculum and leave, to be replaced by others. The administration and the faculty are, in this view, the people who work in the grease pit at a Jiffy Lube, while the students are the line of cars waiting to be serviced. Using the Wal-Mart metaphor, the administration manages the store, while the faculty serves the students, who are, of course, customers.

Actually, that view overlooks the complex interaction of the involved groups. Viewed from a systems perspective, what we have is not a steady line of customers waiting to be served, but a large and complex pattern of interactive relationships and influences. Students and faculty are present for their own reasons, some of which have little to do with learning and teaching; identity reasons are a factor, for example. Each group both influences and is influenced by the others. Each group also establishes both formal and informal, recognized and unrecognized relationships with the other groups. Rather than a top-down operation, as envisioned by the traditional specialist views, we have a system where all parts are roughly equal. Administrators provide directions for programs, true, but then faculty and students decide whether to partake of them or not. For decades, specialist educational researchers have complained that the biggest barriers to the utilization of the principles that they have discovered are the individual classroom teachers. The resistance generally comes about because the changes those principles represent are not morphogenic; they are not perceived as enhancing the system. Should the programs fit the teachers' needs, they will be incorporated into the system. Should they not, they will be resisted. The same fate awaits the initiatives that faculty members construct for students. Faculty make demands of students, who then proceed to make up their minds whether those demands fit their needs or not.

Everyone who works in a community college has heard administrators complain that students reject their initiatives; stories abound of honors programs that have everything but students and the technical and career programs developed by grant money that students refuse to enter. Administrators also complain of the rules they establish for faculty which teachers blithely ignore. Faculty members discuss assignments they can no longer use because students will not complete them, books they can no longer require because students will not - or cannot - read them.

No, a top-down model will not explain the actual workings of the community college. In truth, the operation is an interlocking pattern of mutual influences; one party initiates an action but only after a study that attempts to discover how the other affected system members will receive it. The other parties then have to react and their reaction cannot be fully predicted. In this way, morphogenesis is maintained. A traditional linear examination of the roles played by individuals will not reveal the truth of the situation because it does not consider morphogenesis; the whole makes the determinations, not the parts. Not recognizing this fact can lead to confusion and a lack of clear direction.

Systems maintain themselves in a changing environment. Every system seeks homeostasis, the steady state that allows survival. Each initiative, each movement, creates a perceived threat to the survival of the system which must be tested and, as often as not, resisted. Everyone who labors in the system has seen how instruments of shared governance - faculty senates, for example - can stifle change in an attempt to maintain the status quo. We have also seen how students can subvert faculty and administrative changes; an attempt to deepen a syllabus often meets with a passive-aggressive response that dooms the attempt. Students who do not honor honors programs cause changes in those programs simply by resisting them.

None of these attempts to stifle initiatives are even recognized as efforts to resist change or to maintain homeostasis. People involved in a system will very often perceive their actions as promoting change, even when the effect is the opposite. The goal of morphogenic change is to allow growth while maintaining homeostasis, which is exactly what the people who stifle change believe they are doing. Not recognizing this fact can lead to staggering and ineffective movements in an unclear direction.

Systems create themselves in response to the challenges of the environment. Community colleges evolve by a form of morphogenesis; they do not change so much as they develop structurally and organically. In a time when society is undergoing such rapid and fundamental changes that it is almost impossible to keep up with them, educational structures, including the community colleges, are retrenching.

Indeed, Neil Postman (1979) sees the current retrenchment as their mission:

> Education tries to conserve tradition when the rest of the environment is innovative. Or it is innovative when the rest of society is tradition-bound. It is a matter of indifference whether the society be volatile or static. The function of education is always to offer the counter-argument, the other side of the picture. (p. 20)

To try to change yourself by going in a different direction from the environment is to maintain a false view of homeostasis. As we shall see in the chapter which discusses administration, after the rapid and revolutionary growth of the community college system, we have settled into a cautious and conscious maintenance of the status quo. Systemically, this method of seeking homeostasis is not morphogenic, so it leads in a mistaken direction.

Natural systems are coordinating interfaces in nature's hierarchy. Community colleges exist in an ecological chain. To thrive, they depend on the surrounding environments - educational, social, economic and spiritual - just as those environments depend on them. When the concept of the ecological chain is ignored and the college tries to go its own way, chaos results.

For example, across the nation, roughly fifty percent of incoming community college students require remediation. The reason for this need is simple: due to many complicated factors, some having to do with the schools and some having to do with the students, previous schooling has not done its job. In most cases, the two-year colleges' efforts at remediation are not overwhelmingly successful; few students who enter developmental programs emerge from them to graduate from the institution. One east coast community college studied the success rate of their developmental English program and discovered that, in the eight years the program had been in existence, only one student had gone through the program successfully. (Success was measured by the students' proceeding on to pass the traditional Freshman Composition-Introduction to Literature sequence.)

Fault finding abounds. The colleges continue to claim that the high schools are to blame for the reading and writing deficiencies of the students. The high schools blame the junior highs. What results is one system failing to achieve its goals and placing the blame for that failure on another system which failed earlier. Since neither system recognizes the systemic connection between the them, no progress is made on the prime issue that unites them: removing the problem.

Other college systems get in trouble by adopting programs that will, they believe, attract students *immediately* and satisfy local business concerns of the moment. These programs invariably fail because they do not consider the long-range, morphogenic growth and evolution of the interested systems.

Decisions made and actions taken without a consideration of the pattern of interfacing systems involved will almost always fail. Therefore, these actions, intended to strengthen the schools, have precisely the opposite effect; they actually weaken the community college system.

Communications in Systems. In systems theory, information processing is more complicated than the normal sender-message-receiver structure that dominates linear studies. Because, in a system, communication patterns both reveal and create the nature of the relationship, it is necessary to take a deeper look at the ways the sender-message-receiver model actually operates.

We will briefly review the workings of this model and then extend them.

The sender, of course, is the person who initiates the message. He has a point that he wants to get across to someone else. That point is the message and the person he wants to get it across to is, obviously, the receiver. The key to this triad is that *unless the message actually reaches the receiver and is accepted, no communication has taken place.* This fact is true regardless of the medium through which the message is sent.

Communications studies indicate that far more messages fail to reach receivers than actually do. Our failed attempts at communication greatly outnumber our successes. The reasons for this phenomenal amount of communications failure are many and complex. For this discussion, let us simply acknowledge that the reasons for failure have four points of origin: the sender, the message itself, the receiver, or some combination of the three. A central factor whether a system communicates well or not is the degree of openness; a system characterized by trust and warmth will communicate better than one characterized by distance and distrust.

Systems theory generally identifies and studies three types of communication:

1: Verbal.

Although verbal communication is central in linear operations, in systems it is almost irrelevant. The larger and more complicated a system becomes, the less effective and important verbal communication becomes. When colleges consisted of a president and twenty faculty members, speech may have been an important factor in decision making, but once a formal bureaucracy and a large faculty has been built up, decision making by the process of talking it out is impossible. As Watzlawick, Beavin and Jackson (1967) say, "Indeed, whenever relationship is the central issue in communication, we find that digital (verbal) language is almost meaningless." (p. 63)

2: Non-verbal.

In the popular mind, non-verbal communication refers to kinesics, the study of body movements, gestures and postures as a means of communication, the body of material popularized under the term "body language." In systemic communication, each involved member quickly becomes sensitized to the kinesics of every other member. When a dean makes a speech meant to be inspirational and the listening faculty hears implied threats, then kinesics have become more important than verbal speech; the true message was the one that was *sensed,* not the words which were heard.

We can extend the notion of non-verbal communication to include the major means of communication among large systems, as community colleges have become, the memo. In community colleges today, memos fly about like losing tickets at a race track. The memo is an example of unilateral communication; it is top-down, begins with the sender and ends with the receiver. Unilateral communication is favored by administrators as a way to instruct faculty and staff in matters of policy, expectations and goals and other matters.

Unilateral communication, whatever form it takes, is not reliable. It is received not literally, but through the senses; as a non-verbal form, it carries the kinesic messages of the senders.

Memos are also directive. They are often meant to convey desires that the administration wish to be obeyed. As such they are examples of parent-child communication, which removes power from the receiver. As a result, the memo is often either ignored or perceived as a threat. In either case, the receiver is responding to the kinesics, rather than the text.

3: Context. Contextual communication is crucial to systems. A change in context will change the way a system operates. The relationship a professor has with his students in class, for example, is different from the one he has with them individually in his office. Similarly, a dean speaking in a meeting is different from the same person speaking over a beer. As the system becomes more complex, members become more sensitive to context. For the system to be healthy, for it to maintain morphogenesis, members must interact in more than a single context. If all communication is formal, taking place behind lecterns or by memos, distance between members is opened, along with all of the factors that accompany distance: suspicion, skepticism, mistrust.

Discussion. Since communication is so important to the health of the system, it must be transactional. Communication that is transactional empowers all of the involved parties and carries the best hope that messages will be sent and received accurately. Transactional communication is a reciprocal process in which all parties both initiate and receive messages and make on-going attempts to insure that understanding is total. Under this model communication is two-way instead of top-down. Information travels in both directions and each message influences the next; the sender considers the message she has received before initiating a new one.

If transactional communication is to be present and effective, however, certain basic skills in information processing must be present. The skills most relevant to the systemic communication in community colleges are briefly described below:

Paraphrasing. An administrator sending a memo will tend to believe her meaning is clear and that full understanding will follow. She will probably also believe that appropriate action will proceed from understanding. None of those beliefs is necessarily accurate.

In order to insure that the message has been received clearly, the receiver must be able to paraphrase the message. To be unable to state the meat of the message in one's own words indicates that the message has not been received. Therefore, to paraphrase means, by definition, to demonstrate apprehension of meaning.

A message that has been clearly sent and clearly received is less likely to cause the problems in the systemic functioning that can result from misinterpretation.

Impression checking. The role of emotion in systemic communication is not always understood. People in systems often discover in the messages they receive motives that were not intended by the senders. The tendency to discover motives is more likely to be present in closed systems. On campuses where tension between parties is present, both faculty and administration react to the perceived motives behind a message from the other group more than they do the text; the subtext takes precedence over the text. To be able to check impressions gives the receiver the power to read kinesic clues and interpret them accurately.

Emotional checking. Often the receiver's feelings can influence the accuracy with which he receives the message. When we perceive ourselves to be under a threat, for example, we will tend to interpret a message from a power source in a threatening way. One adjunct described this tendency: "I was really insecure when I started doing this work. When my chair told me it was best to return papers within a week, I took that to mean I wasn't going to be rehired." Because of her insecurity, this professor failed to recognize the neutral context of the information.

Transactional communication is sensitive to these sources of communication errors and works to insure that they do not occur.
It does so by acknowledging and using the following principles of systemic communication:

1: The stated message might not be the actual message. Many times, the true meaning is in the context. The statement "You are doing a wonderful job but two areas of your performance need improvement," may be accurately interpreted in many ways. The text does not convey the total message.

Similarly, a statement such as "We intend to continue being an excellent college" seems clear on its surface. A quick look at the terms the sentence contains, however, will indicate that interpretive problems might exist: what does the term excellent mean in this context? If the receiver does not believe the school is excellent now, if his definition of the term does not match the speaker's, will he be able to accept the statement? How can an institution 'continue' to be what it is not? To many, the core meaning of that statement would be received as "We're going to continue doing what we are doing now."

2: Context determines behavior and communication. The importance of context was underscored several years ago when a federal judge dismissed a lawsuit against a firm based on the fact that it had lied in its advertising. You have to expect lies in advertising, the judge said, that is the nature of the form; therefore a person reading the ad should know to discount the claim. In other words, the context determines what the words actually mean.

In order to determine exactly what is being communicated, then, it is essential to look at the situation in which the message is being sent. Faculty members talk about their students differently in the office than they do in class. College senators communicate differently on the senate floor than they do in committee meetings or over lunch.

The fact that communication involves context is obvious and would not need to be stated if it were not for the fact that people who perceive themselves as powerless are not as sensitive to context as those who view themselves as empowered. The disempowered are the people who believe the ads and are shocked to discover that the product does not literally live up to every word. As we will see, this fact becomes significant when dealing with certain community college populations, such as adjunct faculty.

3: Messages convey subjective truth. A president speaking to his faculty about the wishes of the board is not reporting their wishes; he is instead communicating *his understanding* of their desires. Similarly, a professor lecturing to a class is reporting her own perception of the truth. When two professors discuss the same student in widely differing terms, so that one describes an excellent student while the other reports that bering in a room with this student is the same as being exposed to the spawn of Satan, both are communicating their own versions of the truth.

All communication is interpretation. An open system is one that recognizes the importance of subjective truth and welcomes a wide range of interpretations. A closed one does not.

4: People want to change without having to actually change themselves. When faculty members discuss what terrible shape their campuses are in and how they need to do things differently, what they probably actually want is for everyone else to come around to their way of thinking. They want the institution to be different without them themselves doing any changing.

A dean complaining about the low morale of faculty does not consider the part that he might play in the beating down of morale. He wants the faculty to change, not himself. The same principle is true of professors who complain about how poorly their students perform. They refuse to recognize that performance is systemic; each party's performance is a response to another party's. Just as the dean can raise faculty morale by interacting with them differently, professors can change their students' performance by altering their own.

Psychologists using systems theory recognize that if they want to, say, help an adolescent change her behavior, they must treat this person as though she were already the person they want to help her become. This same principle is true for all systemic interactions; people treated as the people they already are do not change.

5: As long as a system interacts with a problem, it "owns" the problem. A senate cannot debate a bill unless it has that bill. A board cannot discuss an issue unless that issue is before it. A professor cannot complain about student behavior unless he, in some way, allows that behavior. No one can continually discuss an issue unless they are involved with the issue.

Therefore, there is a vested interest in keeping the issue alive. In many ways, the issue is more important than the solution. Community colleges have been discussing the poor abilities of their students from the very beginning. In fact, they have been much more successful at discussing the poor level of student ability than they have at raising it.

6: The issue discussed may not be the real one. At one college, the faculty and administration discussed for two years the board's insistence that they raise productivity. After two years of heightened debate and deteriorating personal and professional relations, they discovered that productivity was not the issue. The real issue was the attitude of the board.

Another example of a false issue might be the problem of the perceived limited ability of community college students. While all of the attention, effort and money is being thrown at developmental programs, the actual issue might be the direction the institution has chosen to pursue.

When the real issue is ignored, diverted by all of the energy being squandered on a false issue, no progress can be made.

7: Treatments attract like treatments. In general, people respond to the type of treatment they receive by giving back the same type of treatment. To perceive oneself as being under attack causes a counterattack; to be yelled at causes yelling in response. Even should the party who responds in kind know that his is an ineffective response, he will tend to justify his behavior rather than change it: "What else could I do? The man was screaming at me."

Unvarying treatment and response introduces an element of instability into a system. Rather than meeting the problem, the parties harden their positions, become rigid and unyielding, like two retail chains driving themselves into bankruptcy trying to compete with the other by chopping prices. To become rigid closes the system, restricting the flow of new communication.

8: Problems indicate a disfunction in the entire system. The common way of identifying and handling a problem is to identify a person as the source and proceed to make statements such as, "Johnson must be made to stop what he's doing," or "Johnson is the problem." In point of fact, Johnson is no more than a convenient symbol. The problem is systemic. Johnson's behavior is a reflection of the behavior he perceives around him; it is a reflection of his subjective truth.

Systems theory states that all behavior, like any other form of communication, is reciprocative. It cannot be looked at in isolation; to isolate it is to distort it, to remove it from its context. Only when the genuine, systemic problem is identified can it be solved.

9: Behavior, therefore, must be viewed as a systems issue. No person in a system can truly act independently. Just as whatever a parent does is created by his interactions with his children and therefore reflects them, so does a teacher's actions reflect his students. Similarly, an administrator's behavior is a measure of how she perceives the people under her supervision.

To improve communication in a system, then, it is necessary to alter perceptions and relationships.

10: For a system to function at its maximal level, leadership is required. Systems always involve change and, as we have seen, the issue of change is a complex one. It cannot be predetermined and ordered, which is, of course, what management does.

Change must be the result of a total systemic transformation, which requires transformational leadership. As we have also seen, people tend to resist change. The common wish is to live in the results of change; to have things changed without being in any way different. The common wish results in a closed system. To recognize the fallacy of the common wish and to create an open system that will be able to bring about a different wish requires leadership.

Systems operate by communication. The quality of their communication determines whether the system will be open and therefore thriving or closed and on its way to entropy and dissolution.

The community college is too original and too important a structure to allow it to fail to be all that it is capable of being. If future studies of the community college are to actually clarify its role and mission, they must be designed and conducted in systemic, rather than specialist, terms.

Chapter 3:

Four Generations of Confusion

We have seen that, like Wal-Mart, the community college became the pervasive force that it is by being democracy in action. In our age of educational tumult, when every daily newspaper carries a story about some sort of turmoil in higher education, the community college is the success story.

Success, however, is a lamp that still has a price tag dangling from its shade. Rather than solving the problems of higher education, the two year college has begun to suffer from its own set of troubles. This book maintains that the community college at this moment stands confused, its role and direction unclear and misunderstood - even by the people who work within it.

At a time when the institution should be celebrating its primacy, the two-year college finds itself in the position of an adolescent, trying on a succession of weakly defined identities in an effort to find out who he is. Why are the colleges so confused about the nature of their identities? The reasons for the current confusion can be found in the institution's history. If we are to understand how the schools landed in the awkward position of identity confusion, it will be necessary to briefly trace the evolution of this peculiar system of ours.

The rise of the community college. Deegan and Tillery (1985) identify four developmental periods, which they call generations, in the history of the community college:

Generation 1: Extension of High School (1900-1930)

Generation 2: Junior College (1930-1950)
Generation 3: Community College (1950-1970)
Generation 4: Comprehensive Community College (1970-current)

Although Deegan and Tillery do not discuss this effect of the institution's growth, when viewed from the perspective of our current point in the evolutionary history, it can be easily seen that each step in this generational development altered the direction, scope and vision of the community college. Its own history turned the institution into the confused entity that it is today. Generational growth has been Janus-faced and has, therefore, made the institution the force it has become in higher education, but it also created the negative aspects that frustrate the system.

An unanticipated result of the growth was the institutional movement from clarity to confusion. A review of the four generations will demonstrate this point.

Generation 1: The nation's first colleges of the seventeenth and eighteenth centuries deliberately chose to model themselves closely on European universities, basing their aims and curricula on those schools. As the giants of higher education at the time, the influential German universities served as the primary model.

That European model, however, did not ultimately meet the needs of the emerging American nation. As early as 1851, the president of the University of Michigan, Henry Tappan, recognized that the German universities, with their emphasis on graduate and specialist education, lacked a common preparatory function. The young people of America, who had been raised in the new and rough territory that comprised this nation, needed that preparation. What was required, Tappan believed, was an American college which would prepare students for the rigors of the university. Although he did not call it that, Tappan argued for a junior college - two years of basic studies beyond high school that would give students the background required to prosper in the specialized departments of the university.

Other higher education administrators took up Tappan's call for preparatory education. In 1884, at Columbia, John W. Burgess declared that the American universities were trying to do too much. Burgess was convinced that no institution could properly handle both general and specialized education. The general education role belonged to colleges, while specialization was more the task of universities. What would serve the nation's learning needs better, he wrote, was another two years of general education before students entered the universities. He felt academies would be the ideal places to provide that two years of instruction. Once more, the idea of a junior college was floated.

It is important to realize that none of the men advocating the two-year college was truly enamored of either the junior college concept or of general education; their interest lay more in protecting the university's specialization functions. Their intent was to remove students who, they felt, could not benefit from upper division studies.

William Rainey Harper at the University of Chicago, who agreed with the idea of getting the unclean youth of America's heartland out of university as soon as possible, gave the idea a name: the junior college. Like Tappan and Burgess before him, Harper was more a believer in the university than a proponent of the junior colleges; he was concerned with strengthening the University of Chicago's specialist studies, rather than with more wide-ranging and basic general knowledge. The teaching of general knowledge, he felt, was the role of the freshman and sophomore years' study. It belonged to the lower or collegiate division, while specialization belonged to the upper or university division.

Harper's method for strengthening the upper division was simple; he would restrict access, ridding the upper division of students that, to his mind, did not belong there. Many students, he wrote in 1901, continued beyond the first two years although their "best interests would have been served by withdrawal from college" (12) Many
continued because of the stigma that quitting would bring. If these students received a diploma, the stigma would be removed and they would be able to leave honorably. Their departure would allow the university division to concentrate their efforts on students of "the very highest character." (12)

The University of Chicago, therefore, began offering an associates degree at the conclusion of the first two collegiate years.

The rise of the mechanical age, with its accompanying shift from the familiar agricultural to a factory culture, along with the resulting shift of the population from rural to urban areas, caused the idea of the two-year degree to spread quickly. The early twentieth century was a time of great public school expansion, resulting in an overcrowding of colleges and universities. To ease the pressure, high schools began offering post-secondary courses of study which were accepted for transfer at the major universities. As a result, separate junior colleges soon emerged. (The first had already been established in Joliet, Illinois, in 1901.) The growth of the junior college was swift so that, by the close of the first generation, the institution was established.

These early schools were clearly extensions of high school, in many cases using the same buildings and teachers. Certainly, the high schools provided the administrative and funding models that were used.

Discussion. The significant facts about the development of the first generation of community colleges are these:

(1) They were designed to remove students from the universities, to shut the doors rather than open them wider. A system of junior colleges would enable the universities to remain elitist in their basic orientation. In the minds of the universities, the two year colleges were a different animal.

(2) The two-year schools were designed to be something other than colleges and universities. Perhaps they would be less than colleges and universities. Certainly, they would be *different*. In the minds of the university administrators such as Harper, the junior colleges would serve inferior students. Therefore, they were conceived of, at least in the minds of most advocates of the more traditional university system, as inferior institutions.

(3) They were seen, even by their creators, as extensions of high school. This view simply followed the only available logic: since there were only two models, the high school and the university, and the community college was not to be modeled on the university, it had to be seen as related to the high schools. This placement, of course, had serious affects on the prestige of the institution.

The community colleges then, were born with an assigned sense of inferiority. As an institution, they went on to internalize that classification, developing somewhat of an inferiority complex.

Generation Two. Not many American institutions enjoy being viewed as inferior. Even as they internalized the judgment, the junior colleges fought against accepting it. The second generation immediately began to chafe under the weight of the assigned sense of inferiority and determined to do something about it. Assuming that it was the identification with high school that caused them to be viewed as inferior institutions, Generation Two schools threw off the high school model. The second generation was characterized by the shift from a secondary to a collegiate stance.

Social and economic conditions did not permit the shift to be completed; the depression brought a demand for low cost schooling, causing enrollments to grow dramatically. The crashing economy also added a new function to the schools: occupational retraining. As the depression threw people out of work, the community colleges saw a role for themselves that, while it did not mesh with the collegiate stance they were trying to adopt, still had the benefit of not emanating from or resonating with the high schools. Job retraining programs proliferated as the people whose lives were thrown out of alignment by the depression came to the community colleges to learn the new skills they hoped would align them once more.

Still bothered by the association with the high schools, the faculty and administrators of the Generation Two schools created a new movement toward professionalism. By 1930, some 259 of these institutions were operating, enough to enable professional organizations such as the American Association of Junior Colleges to emerge. Despite the fact that much of their growth had little to do with the collegiate function, the growth caused teachers, staff and administrators to identify themselves with colleges and universities, rather than with high schools. As the second generation proceeded, the notion of the community college as an extension of high school disappeared. Indeed, as early as the second annual meeting of the American Association of Junior Colleges in 1922, the junior college was defined as "an institution offering two years of instruction of strictly collegiate grade." (Baker 1994)

Administrative control over the institutions shifted from high school boards to a combination of state and county higher education commissions. From the beginning, however, the colleges were characterized by one of the things that has been a continuing and dominant factor in the rise of community colleges: local control, a factor we will discuss in more detail when the examination turns to administration and governance. For now, we need only recognize that control remained close to the people. The colleges were often responsible to a district or a county, rather than a state.

Even in states such as California, which operated the institutions under state control, local boards dominated and had high degrees of autonomy.

During the second generation, the mission of the community college had become solidified. Deegan and Tillery identify six factors which defined the mission: (1) terminal education, (2) general education, (3) transfer and career orientation and guidance, (4) lower-division preparation for university transfer, (5) adult education, and (6) removal of matriculation deficiencies. These areas remain dominant today.

If any single area dominated, though, it was the transfer program. As the schools became established as separate entities and broke off their connections with high schools, they identified with and articulated with upper division colleges and universities. By the close of the second generation, the schools had successfully shaken off their image as extensions of high school. For all practical purposes, the formerly scorned schools had successfully come to be viewed as institutions of higher learning. Exactly what kind of higher education they featured, however, is debatable.

Discussion. During generation two, the community college (1) adopted local control, (2) became professionalized, (3) shook off its identification with the high schools, substituting instead an identification with the colleges and universities, and (4) adopted the elements that still identify its current mission.

In Generation two, then, the colleges had an opportunity to create their own identity, to become the separate and distinct entities that, in a morphogenic sense, they already were. The prevailing logic of the time caused them to miss that opportunity.

Instead, they made a sensical move and then immediately followed it up with a nonsensical one: they rejected the high school model, and then decided to model themselves on the universities who had already declared them inferior schools for inferior students. They became the educational equivalent of the young man who continues to beg for a date with the most popular girl in school, even though she has made it clear that she'll never believe him worthy of her time, attention and affection.

The begging was based on a fundamental mistaken perception, which is the idea that the community college prepared freshmen and sophomores for transfer. In reality, the community college is not simply the first two years of the university. By adopting its student-centered policies and striving to guarantee equal access for everyone, the two-year college assured that it would never just reflect the lower division of the university.

The institution does what that lower division does, but it also does *more*. Systemically, the institution is radically different and the difference was already apparent during the period of generation two. But during that time, the people who were building and staffing the schools could not recognize their uniqueness, so the institution operated on a false model, basing itself on something it was not. As a consequence, it never truly recovered from the initial perception of inferiority that had been cast upon it by the university administrators who conceived of the two-year college as a sort of academic dumping ground.

In the eyes of far too many, that sense of inferiority still persists.

Generation Three. The third generation was characterized by growth and expansion. Impressed by the success of the second generation, state and local governments pumped more money into the two-year colleges. For much of the decade of the sixties, a new community college opened each week. As new campuses were being built, existing ones expanded. So did the programs and curricula. During this generation, the phrase "open-door" became a rallying cry and open admissions became the operating policy for most schools.

Rapid expansion created new tensions; in the third generation, for example, the colleges began to take the transfer function for granted. Rather than building on their major success, they tried to transform themselves into institutions that truly served *everyone.* In the third generation, these schools truly became colleges of the community, offering the something for everyone that Robert Hutchins decried. The movement toward Wal-Mart had begun.

The direction of national politics served as an impetus. In 1950, Harry Truman, the guiding force behind this transformation, created the President's Commission on Higher Education - Expansion of Educational Opportunity. Truman declared in a letter that he was

> particularly interested in knowing more about efforts to reduce geographic and economic barriers to the development of individual talents through extended educational opportunities which seem to be reflected in many states and localities by so-called "community colleges." (Quoted in Deiner, 130)

The charge to Truman's commission was to make a comprehensive study of community colleges in order to determine whether the government could use these schools to more adequately create equal educational opportunity.

The commission determined that community colleges could indeed be used to equalize opportunity and recommended that both the number of community colleges and their activities be increased. Under the Truman plan, the public two-year colleges would continue to be locally controlled and would provide "educational service to the whole community." This purpose, the commission stated

> will require of it a variety of functions and programs. It will provide college education for the youth of the community certainly, so as to remove geographic and economic barriers to educational opportunity and discover and develop individual talents at low cost and easy access. But in addition, the community college will serve as an active center of adult education. It will attempt to meet the total post-high school needs of its community. (U.S. President's Commission, p. 48)

To meet those needs, the commission recommended that community colleges "emphasize programs of terminal education." (68) As examples of the types of offerings the colleges would provide, the report postulated that

> if the community could be improved by teaching restaurant managers something about the bacteria of food, the community college sets up such a course and seeks to enroll as many of those employed in food service as it can muster. If the community happens to be a center for travelers from Latin America, the college provides classes in Spanish for salespeople, waitresses, bellboys and taxicab drivers. (70)

The Truman Commission created a growth explosion. At the same time, the commission changed the function of the schools irrevocably. Henceforth

(1) transfer programs would be simply one of many offerings to the community;

(2) the college would serve whoever could benefit, whether that service resulted in a diploma and led to continued study at a university or not;

(3) The college would serve whoever showed up at its doors, regardless of academic qualifications. Everyone, the theory declared, would benefit from some program or course offered;

(4) The college would try to be all things to all people, offering whatever the community required or desired. Academic value would not be a determiner of the value of a program or course.

Discussion. During the third generation, the community college began to become the victim of its own success. It had proven that it could perform its basic junior college function well and went on to poke its finger into many pies. The Truman Commission simply spurred growth in a direction the colleges had already chosen; it extended their function. The problem was that the Commission did not simply widen the mission of the community college; instead it removed the borders. The doors were not so much opened as ripped off of their hinges.

In so doing, the Truman Commission inadvertently created a systemic wrench that challenged the capacity of the community college system to survive. As stated earlier, all systems have boundaries, that is, patterns and values which characterize the system and give it its particular identity. The system uses boundaries to determine who is or is not a member, in that way restrict the information coming into the system. A system that allow a large amount of information to enter is described as open; similarly, one which restricts information is said to be closed.

Should a system accept too much information, openness turns into chaos. Its boundaries will "become indistinct and [the system] will not be discernable as separate from any other system." (Becvar & Becvar, 1982,

p. 11) The morphogenetic nature of the whole institution will suffer and its survival may, as a result, be threatened. The demands placed on the boundaries by the Truman Commission seriously weakened the boundaries of the community college.

One campus became the home for many levels of education, as colleges reinterpreted the Commission's findings and constructed ambitious programs as a result. The commission's view of a course designed to teach bacteria control to restaurant managers - a one shot offering - quickly became a restaurant management curriculum, complete with a sixty credit degree requirement (or a thirty credit certificate.) Other non-academic offering proliferated, so that everything from a pre-medicine major to truck driver training was available at the same address. The challenge for the community college was to provide this level of service while maintaining the boundaries that gave it its unique identity.

The two-year colleges also tried to adapt too quickly, in a fashion that was not morphogenic. They tried to become what their public desired, while not requiring anything of that public. For a public institution to serve the public is, of course, to provide a genuine benefit, but for a school to truly provide a service to its public, it must make demands of that public. To benefit from educational ventures, for example, it must be necessary for a student to be able to read and write and exercise personal initiative. The community colleges quickly learned that a large percentage of the new students created by the programs and course offerings that grew out of the Truman Commission's recommendations did not have a simple grasp of basic literacy.

Rather than ask that these people equip themselves in the adult education centers the commission had asked the colleges to house, the way parents ask children to wash their hands before eating, most of the colleges decided to try to accomplish two goals simultaneously: to equip the students to be able to partake of the bounty at the very time they were partaking of it. The children would wash their hands *while eating*. They would try to become literate while simultaneously trying to make it through an academic program. This almost impossible goal, which still troubles most schools, grew out of a misinterpretation of the Truman Commission's recommendations. The language of the report indicates that the commission meant for the schools to provide housing for the non-academic offerings, to make them available to the audience that could benefit from them, while continuing to provide the traditional junior college curriculum.

If the community needed bakers, the commission said, a community college could train them. The commission, however, did not demand that the schools transform the potential bakers into academically capable, degree-seeking college students. The colleges, because of reasons that were not always learning-driven, reasons that often had to do with how the colleges were funded, made that decision on their own.

According to the commission, academic and non-academic programs could exist side by side. They did not, however, have to unite. This fundamental act of misinterpretation had serious results which continue to this day. In fact, the misinterpretation that created the confusion in Generation Three evolved into the basic operating philosophy for Generation Four. It was during this generation of community college history that the systemic boundaries truly became indistinct.

Generation Four. Deegan and Tillery labelled this generation the age of the comprehensive community college. We could just as easily call it the age of the identity crisis. If the Truman doctrine expanded the schools, it also contributed to the tendency toward confusing their charter. No longer would the schools have a solid core identity, no longer would they be able to claim a single unifying mission which would serve to unite the various divisions and departments. Instead the two year colleges would simply provide a central location for many divergent activities. They would, in reality, be many learning centers gathered in a central location. The campuses would resemble the inside of a Wal-Mart, a single complex with many aisles and shelves where a huge amount of products, which may or may not have anything in common, could be found.

This idea of many functions at one address was complicated by the changing educational needs of the nation. For most of our history, education was looked upon as a finite process; one achieved a degree, looked upon education as a part of the past and entered the work force.

During the seventies and eighties, the years of generation four, that notion died. The long-predicted age of lifelong learning became a reality. The expanded educational opportunities that had caused the transformation of the junior college into the comprehensive community college created more college graduates. With more and better educated candidates to choose from, business and industry had their pick of the field and, as a result, were able to demand better educated workers. Rapid increases in technology caused more changes. More people returned to school for both degree work and specialized training in precise areas. Even workers in skilled trades, such as mechanics, who once learned by doing, now engaged in formal training as computerization put an end to the idea of the shade tree mechanic.

Most of these increased demands for further learning were satisfied by community colleges. Access to perpetual learning opportunities became the their rallying cry. Students came to them to acquire job entry skills, job retraining, career enhancement skills, cultural enrichment, and movement toward personal goals, as well as to accumulate credits for transfer to a university.

At the same time they coped with all of these new types of students, community colleges continued to offer a second chance to unprepared students of all ages and backgrounds, most of whom did not fit traditional academic demographics. Likely to be the first in their families to attend college, they were older, more often than not attending the schools on a part-time basis while establishing families and careers.

In keeping with the thinking that emerged in the third generation, no qualifications were demanded of those who entered. Should a learning need arise or should an opportunity present itself, the generation four comprehensive community college viewed it as their solemn obligation to provide whatever would satisfy it.

Discussion. As a result of the fourth generation's educational sprawl

(1) the colleges lost their leadership role. Instead of providing a model that students would adapt themselves to and that faculty and administrators would use as a guide, the colleges tried to adapt themselves to the needs of their students. They followed rather than leading. The trend toward offering much while demanding little intensified.

(2) The schools became less rigorous. Remedial offerings grew as the number of academically unprepared increased. Since the colleges continued to ignore the one-shot offering, preferring to place students in diploma-track programs, graduation requirements were rewritten and softened. Advanced courses designed to transfer to four year institutions were eliminated as requirements so that more pragmatic functional courses could be fit into a sixty credit program.

(3) It became difficult to generalize about students. In some schools, fewer than 2% transferred to universities, while in others, more than 90% did. Some campuses resembled four year colleges; others resembled trade schools. All community colleges, though, prided themselves on the open-door, their closeness to the community and their responsiveness to student needs. As a result, when discussions were held about "the student body," the talk lacked a unifying focus, since each participant had a different mental image of the people being discussed. Fewer truly valuable initiatives could be tried because of a lack of clear agreement on who the

receivers of the initiatives - the students - were.

(4) Partly because of the increased competition for traditional students caused by a tightening economy, community colleges made great efforts to recruit new populations. The non-traditional student became a greater force in the community college vision. Recent immigrants, returning adult women, handicapped adults, minorities and other special populations grew. At the same time, the crashing economy caused a return of the traditional student, but in many cases, on a part-time basis.

So much growth in so many areas further confused the issue of who the schools served. Additionally, so much growth in a time of entrenched budgets diffused the efforts of many of the colleges, leading to the frequent complaint that the community college had lost its direction in an effort to be all things to all people.

(5) No one could any longer say with certainty exactly what the community college was. In fact, few could agree on what it *should* be. For a program director in Mortuary Science, the college is an entirely different place than it is for the chair of the Art department.

In generation four, much of the growth of the institution was not morphogenic. It did not grow organically out of the direction earlier generations had provided. In fact, each generation clouded the issue by defining itself and its mission differently and, as often as not, in negative terms; each was better at saying what the community colleges were not than what they were. To a generation one administrator, the community college was not a university. A generation two manager insisted his school was not an extension of high school. For generation three, it was not a trade school but for generation four, it was not to be restricted by any single definition.

With no clear unifying vision, much of the growth simply happened in response to unpredictable conditions. The schools were reactive rather than proactive and to react is to be in a powerless position, the victim of events beyond one's control. Lacking a clear vision of itself and its role, the community college reacted to each situation as it came up without a comprehensive plan to determine its way of reacting. Most of the schools have mission statements but in many cases these statements do not guide because they are too vaguely stated and generalized. Many also do not serve because once they are written, they are roundly ignored and never consulted again. As Lorenzo (1994) has pointed out, a failure to internalize the results of a mission study "may result in a mission review's falling short of its best possible outcome." (121)

As a result of all of the above factors, the fourth generation could be viewed as the generation of management, rather than leadership. According to Benis and Nanus (1985) leadership is causative; it can invent and create. It is morally purposive and can lead to higher degrees of consciousness. Leadership, therefore, can transform institutions and the people in them. Management, on the other hand, "Typically consists of a set of contractual exchanges, 'you do this job for this reward.'" (218) Where leadership goes forward, management marches in place.

At this writing, while the fourth generation marches in place, the fifth generation of community college history is coming into being. It will be essential for the fifth generation to find a sense of direction and proclaim a defined mission that can be accomplished. So far, however, the emerging fifth generation is characterized by both its own confusion and the residual confusion of the fourth generation. The purpose, direction, scope - indeed the very future of America's most promising educational institution - is in flux.

If the fifth generation cannot remove the confusion, what will become of the community colleges?

Chapter Four:

The Faculty

We will begin with a profile:
In order to be ready for his eight o'clock class, Mark usually hits the office by seven-thirty in the morning on Mondays, Wednesdays and Fridays. Since he is often the first person to arrive, he walks back to the lounge area and makes a pot of coffee. If he has any copies to make, he uses the zerox machine while the coffee brews. Then, a cup in hand, he strolls back to his office and checks his notes.

He has three classes today: back to back freshman compositions and, after an office hour in which he must be available to students, an introduction to literature. He is concerned about his eight o'clock composition class. "The other two are all right. They're coming along, showing some promise, but this one...." His voice trails off and he shakes his head sadly.

Since the class has a cause-effect paper due this week, Mark intends to spend the morning teaching an essay that has particularly good causal analysis in it. "What's going to happen is that only half the class will have read it and half of them won't understand it." He scans the essay again, making marginal notes. "You don't usually get a class where even the threat of a quiz won't make them read, but it happens every once in a while. This is one of them."

Mark recognizes that he is partially at fault. "It's funny but a class dynamic builds up really fast and you've got to shape it carefully because once that dynamic is in place, it's hell to change it. This one got a poor dynamic immediately. I guess I didn't control it enough in the beginning. Half the people in class are failing and they don't seem to care." He shakes his head again. "I just don't understand it. I'll never understand it."

He and his fellow teachers find themselves speaking of their own undergraduate days quite often, discussing the ways in which the teaching-learning situation has changed since then. Most of the changes they identify are negative and the conversations always end with the sentence, "We'd never have done what they do."

"We sound like a bunch of geezers," Mark says.

With twenty-five years on the job, he is aware of his status as a veteran. "People come to me for advice now," he says wonderingly. "It feels like it was only last week when I was asking my colleagues how to handle stuff. Worse yet, I find myself offering advice without being asked. I'll overhear somebody talking about a problem and start suggesting ways to deal with it off the top of my head. I can do that because I've seen damn near everything."

When he reaches the eight o'clock class, it contains no surprises; it goes as badly as he expected it to. "All of the people I expected to be unprepared were unprepared. Nobody is comfortable with the principles of causation; they accept coincidence, false causes, rationalizations, all of that, without even questioning it. I try to teach them to be intellectually skeptical, to challenge all statements and all uses of language, but they just don't get it. They don't recognize what the careless use of language can do."

He decides that he will have to work in some material on General Semantics. If the students understand more about how the language operates, he figures, maybe they will be more sensitive to its uses.

The next class, also a freshman composition and also dealing with causation, goes more smoothly. "It's funny. Same objectives, same material, radically different results. It would be easy to say it's the students, but I'm afraid that would be facile. It's the whole interaction. They're different people from the other class, completely different, and I'm different when I'm with them. I'll have to rethink what I'm doing in the other class."

After the class, a steady stream of students comes in to see him during his office hour. He is a well-known and popular teacher. "No big thing," he says, explaining his popularity, "it comes from being around forever." Students like to drop by to chat, "to chill." Others come in to discuss assignments or to go over previous work, in order to learn how to avoid making the same errors in the future. Some are there only to argue about grades. This one is a pleasant hour that passes quickly. Marc has to chase away a student in order to go to his next class.

The story he assigned for the intro to lit class goes over pretty well, he feels. "I try to be careful to pick stuff that relates to their lives without being patronizing. I mean, I don't go looking for simple stuff with teenaged heroes or anything like that, but I do look for stuff that has heavy internal conflicts revolving around moral choices and tough decisions in situations they can relate to."

Today's story, Camus' "The Guest" fits the criteria, since it involves a question of loyalties, asking whether your personal moral position takes precedence over your duty and loyalty to the state. The discussion is lively and Mark enjoys it. He comes away feeling that the class is learning to ask tough questions and to think more clearly about them. "When I see that questioning reflected in their writing, though, then I'll be happy."

After class, he returns to his office and lunches on a sandwich and more coffee. Although this isn't a formal office hour, his students know he can usually be found in the office and they drop by. On this day, a young woman getting ready to transfer to an out-of-state university stops in to ask for a letter of recommendation. Mark agrees to write it. As she is leaving, a former student, now enrolled in one a colleague's American Literature section asks him to read and react to a paper she is getting ready to submit to the other professor. After cautioning her that he is not fully aware of the values being sought by the other professor, Mark agrees. He reads over the paper and makes a few editorial suggestions. He is careful to praise the solid qualities of the writing before suggesting changes.

"I'll never tell a student what to write or lay down a bunch of rules. Especially if it's a student in someone else's class. Good writing is a discovery process and I don't want to take the discovery away from the student. I will, though, take an existing piece of work and suggest ways to make it clearer or deeper. I'll suggest general principles and let the student discover the specifics."

By the time he has finished, it is time for his committee meeting. Mark serves on the assessment and placement committee, whose job it is to examine the way the reading, writing, and math skills of entering students are tested and how they are assigned to classes on the basis of that assessment. "I was excited about joining this committee because it's such a vital action. Students who are placed in classes they can't handle are going to fail, it's as simple as that. You want students to succeed, you've got to put them in the proper classes."

Mark's excitement didn't last, though. He has worked with this group for two years, attending bi-weekly meeting and claims that they have accomplished nothing. "This year, we've spent the entire year researching the perfect computer system for assessment. We have considered and rejected a hundred programs. What makes it an exercise in futility is that the school does not have the money to buy any new program. If we found the perfect program for six bucks, we couldn't buy it and all of us on the committee knew this all year. I kept asking if anything would come of this work and the committee chair kept saying, "well, maybe they'll find the money somewhere,' even though we all knew damn well they wouldn't. This was the charge the committee was given, he said, we were going to carry out the charge whether anything came of it or not." He shakes his head again. "Never join a committee that's dominated by counselors and staff people. They have to be here till five o'clock and having a meeting beats working."

The meeting runs until four and then Mark packs up his briefcase and heads home. Tonight, he will drive to the state university where he is taking courses toward his doctorate. Tomorrow, he will do it all again.

Three Categories of Faculty. It would be easy to think of Mark as a "typical" community college faculty member but such a characterization would probably not be accurate; the typical faculty member does not exist. It is difficult to speak of the faculty with any degree of accuracy because the systemic nature of the community college has caused the creation of three separate and distinct faculties: academic, vocational and adjunct. Although all three types work with students in an attempt to reach educational ends, they are not united; in fact, not even the educational ends they pursue are the same. The fact that each of the three faculties plays a different role in the system, coupled with the fact that each systemic role is to some degree in conflict with the others means that, on some issues, at least, the faculties will be in conflict with each other.

Inevitably, each of these faculty groups view the colleges differently. Therefore, the needs, views, status and perceptions of the individual members - not to mention the overall collective vision - differ among these three categories. Indeed, not even the mission looks the same when viewed by the separate groups. As a result, the tendency to examine the community college faculty as a single whole, which has guided most of the past investigations, is not adequate. The differences are too striking.

Despite the difficulties, a systemic examination demands that the nature and the role of the faculty not be ignored. A close look at the three faculties will show that each influences the overall system - including the other faculty groups - and each is, in turn, influenced by the system as a whole. These interfacing influences, of course, can be either positive and negative.

Faculty and personal power. The story of the three faculties is the story of a perceived decline in personal power for two of the three groups, with a third group denied power under any circumstances. This chapter explores

that move to disempowerment. To aid the exploration, we will focus on the way the academic and technical faculties view the following issues:
1: Faculty commitment to the community college vision.
2: The tasks of the faculty.
3: Causes of the perceived loss of personal power.
4: The changing student body.

This chapter will concentrate primarily on full-time academic and technical-vocational faculty. Adjuncts, because they face additional problems all their own, will be covered in the following chapter.

Faculty commitment to the community college mission. Although the mission of the community colleges has been referred to in previous pages, to discuss faculty commitment to that mission it is at this point necessary to make discussion of the mission more explicit.

As far back as 1962, during the rapid expansion that was the hallmark of the third generation, Fields isolated and identified five characteristics that he saw as unique to community colleges:
1: Democratic.

The schools offered low tuition and fees and easy access. They established and maintained non-selective, open-attendance policies. They were accessible both geographically and socially and were designed to offer a wide-range of educational opportunities to the largest number of people.
2: Comprehensive.

As a result of the easy access and the expanding educational opportunities which were increasing in the larger society at the time, the community colleges attracted a broad range of students who demonstrated a bafflingly wide scope of abilities, aptitudes and interests. To serve these students, the colleges developed comprehensive curriculums. Since the needs of the students were broad, so were the programs.
3: Community-centered.

As previously stated, a goal of the colleges was to develop the community at large, to provide a social service by increasing the educational level of the community. Because they were locally supported and controlled, utilizing local resources for educational purposes, the community colleges were chartered to play the role of developer of the intellect of the city or county in which the schools were located.
4: Dedicated to Life-long Education.

Four year schools provided a form of terminal education; once the students achieved the degrees they pursued, they left the institution. At the community college, programs for individuals of all ages, manifesting all manner of educational needs were offered. Although degrees were offered, many students did not pursue them; some already held diplomas and were present for specialized learning based upon their interests, while others did not see the acquisition of a diploma as central to their life goals at the time of study.

At the two-year college, options were wider and more varied. Instead of pursuing a straight line to a destination, the community colleges allowed students to stroll along rambling paths.

5: Adaptable.

As every presidential administration since Harry Truman's noted, four-year schools were rigid, as firmly fixed in their paths as an arrow. Should the university student's needs change, he could be forced to change his field of study - and perhaps his place of study. The community college, however, was flexible, able to adapt to the changing needs of its clientele and the changing needs of society. If the universities were arrows, community colleges were shotguns.

While essentially agreeing with Fields, O'Banion (1972) slightly altered the characteristics. In his view, community colleges were (1) open-door, (2) comprehensive, (3) community-oriented, (4) student- centered, (5) innovative, and (6) noted for emphasizing teaching.

These are the core ideas that make up the paradigm that the system operates under; these ideas are the commonly depicted portrait of the community college's reality. These core ideas, of course, contribute to the Wal-Mart image. They also blur the system's boundaries.

Faculty acceptance of the mission. If, no matter whose descriptors are used, these are the characteristics that define the mission of the community college, then it is reasonable to expect that faculty members would accept and uphold them. Several early studies (Cohen & Brawer, 1972; Cross, 1976; Garrison, 1968) demonstrate that this expectation has traditionally been met. These studies declare that teachers have been on board.

The literature maintains that community college faculties are student-centered and community-oriented, innovative, flexible and open-minded. Moreover, they are most often described as being committed to the philosophies and practices of the community college.

Yet, viewed through a slightly more focused lens, these seemingly positive reports contain a few disturbing breaks in the solid walls of the paradigm. As far back as 1973, for example, Leslie studied the faculty's commitment to the community college philosophy in more detail and found that even at that time, at the beginning of the fourth generation of community college history, when the shift toward a more comprehensive vision was in its first flourishing, the level of commitment was not very deep. Leslie described it as a reserved agreement.

The strongest agreement with the described mission was found among three subdivisions of faculty. Younger faculty, those without doctorates and faculty working in vocational-technical programs were most committed to the traditional view of the mission. The opposites of these categories - older faculty, those holding the doctoral degree and those whose teaching assignments were in the liberal arts - were most likely to question the mission.

A disagreement over acceptance of the college's mission indicates a difference in the very definition of what a community college is and should be. The fact that such a disagreement exists between academic and vocational-technical faculty shows that a schism has developed between these teaching groups. As we shall see, this schism has profound systemic implications.

The Task of the Faculty. The teaching faculty is the key to the community college's work. Other factors in the system, such as the support staff, administrators, politicians and students, might help draw up the route for the trip, but it is the faculty members who drive the bus. They decide the content of the course, the intellectual level of the material and the approach to it. Teachers select the texts and supporting materials, decide how to get the material across to the students, determine the sequence of the learning, as well as the means of discovering what learning has taken place. To use the Wal-Mart analogy, the teaching faculty places the order for the merchandise, stocks the shelves, meets the customers and determines the strategy for this particular sale and guides the customers to the best purchase to meet their needs.

Viewed systemically, teaching is no easy task. A professor oversees a very complicated transaction -- helping students acquire not simply facts, details and skills, but ideas, concepts, values, relationships, and approaches to both current and future learning. Should the educational transaction be successful, the students are different people at the end than they were in the beginning. Not only do they know more, they *are* more.

Significantly, it is not the teacher who succeeds but the student. The faculty member's goal is to contribute to the success. She cannot, however, claim it; it never belongs to her. When a student achieves his goals, the teacher has also achieved hers, but she lives with the knowledge that she is simply a tool a student uses.

Since, as the continuing discussion will show, success in the community college is an elusive concept, the job of the faculty member, especially in a shifting educational paradigm, is almost impossible.

The changing systemic paradigm has created profound changes in the way the job is done. One veteran professor currently assigned to the teaching of developmental English classes remarked, "When we first put these classes together twenty years ago, the students we placed in them were so much better than they are now. Nowadays, the students we used to place in remedial classes would qualify for standard classes. The quality of students has gotten that much lower."

The head of the English department in another community college stated bluntly, "I'm running a developmental English service. That's all."

Vocational and technical faculty see the situation differently because they are not as effected by the paradigm; they have not experienced a decline. A teacher in an agricultural program in a rural community college said succinctly, "My students are excellent and are getting better every year. I have no complaints."

"Of course his students are excellent," said a psychology professor in response. "He can pre-screen and select. Funny, around here you have to qualify to study farming but not to study psychology. I have to take whoever walks in the door. You've also got to figure he doesn't ask them to write anything. Not a single paper or essay exam. If his students had to write papers, I wonder what he'd say."

Among academic faculty, there is a widespread feeling that students in technical and vocational programs are somehow not *real* students. The feeling sometimes extends to the people who guide them: vocational-technical teachers are not seen as *real* faculty. Similarly, among the vocational-technical instructors, a feeling exists that teachers of academic subjects are elitists. "Those Humanities guys think they're better than everybody else," said one teacher in a truck driving program. "They can't actually *do* anything but, boy, can they tell you how stuff ought to be done."

In discussing academic faculty, vocational teachers repeatedly use the phrase "real world" in a disparaging way. "Get those guys out in the real world," one said, "and they wouldn't last an hour." Another echoed him: "They just know theory. They don't know a thing about the real world."

The two faculties are the academic equivalent of feuding brothers in a family. Both fear the family is becoming more dysfunctional and each is quick to blame the other for the disappearance of healthy functioning.

For academic faculty, the story of the community college has been the slow drift from mission to disillusionment, from boutique to Wal-Mart, a drift that has moved them from a position of power to a lack of perceived power.

"When I first came here," one philosophy professor declared, "the technical guys were asking us to help them survive. Now, we're asking them for help."

As one veteran Art teacher said, "We used to count for something around here. Now, in the eyes of everybody - other teachers, students, the administration - the Humanities are the problem, not the solution."

Powerlessness in Academic Faculty. The art teacher's remark reveals a perceived lack of power, which is characteristic of academic faculty. Like the adolescent brother who fights with his older sibling because he feels estranged from his parents and believes his brother gets all of the attention, academic faculty members feel misunderstood and overlooked. The teachers feel that the systemic growth of the community college, the move toward comprehensiveness, has been achieved at their expense.

Academic faculty's movement from empowerment to a lack of power has its origins in two concurrent trends: (1) their own aging process, and (2) the slowdown in the growth of the community colleges during the fourth generation. As growth decreased, the average age of the faculty increased. Cohen and Brawer (1987) argue that age distribution has changed the very nature of the job for older faculty. That change has greatly affected their level of commitment to the mission of the community college.

According to their studies, younger faculty had a greater commitment to the traditional community college mission; they were closer to the students, spent more time with them outside of class and were more conscious of the qualities they wanted students to gain. Older faculty were shown to be more involved with the managerial aspects of the job; over the years of their tenure, they drifted into committee work, spent more time in community service, took on more responsibilities to their professional associations, conducting research on teaching and other roles outside the classroom.

Seidman (1985) quotes one veteran teacher:

> I serve on the curriculum ... and long-range planning committee of the college. I feel like I attend a tremendous number of meetings.... I would say the majority of time it is irritating for me because I don't feel we're dealing with the problems.... That is, you know, what is the purpose of the school? (25)

Ironically, many of the faculty rendered powerless by the move to comprehensiveness owe their jobs to that movement. A great number of them entered the system during the third generation, when the community college was still a noble experiment. As the fourth generation brought on a stabilization and the colleges responded to a period of slow growth by spreading their energies into the non-traditional paths that comprehensiveness demanded, these instructors found their sense of mission - and their own sense of usefulness - diminished. As a result, their feeling of empowerment declined.

These older faculty members also found their disciplines and specialties under attack. As the shift toward more comprehensive programs gained strength, academic professors looked on in horror as their courses were dropped from curricular paths in order to make room for vocational and technical offerings. The schism between faculty groups widened.

Because of a natural aging process and a changing educational mission, these people were no longer the restless innovators of their youth. One described himself as

> An "exhausted insurgent." That's me. I'm an exhausted insurgent and I've had it. How did I get that way? Age.... When the institution was younger and new, there were a lot of things we figured we could get done.... The institution is a lot bigger; it's much harder to get things done. (Seidman, 43-44)

Many teachers, such as this one, no longer saw restless innovation as a rewarding practice. Demoralized by the changes going on around them, they looked around the campus on which they spent their adult working lives, no longer recognized it and retreated from it.

One veteran History professor described his own demoralization by saying,

> I agree with the research that says younger faculty are closer to the students. To my experience, that's true. The only thing the researchers missed are the reasons. The younger guys haven't gotten jaded yet the way the rest of us have. They haven't been around long enough to learn that, as far as our students go, you're not going to make any silk purses out of cow's ears.

The Changing Student Body. Another factor in the disenchantment of academic faculty is the change in another part of the system, the student body. An alteration of one aspect of the system creates a systems push that requires an adjustment; the other elements in the overall system must adjust to the new configuration; academic faculty has, on the whole, been slow to make the necessary changes. Indeed, many argue that the students are the ones who need to change, not the faculty.

Changing the mission of the college changed the student body, creating new and different responsibilities for the faculty. Professors had to work with students who were less likely to be prepared, who were often poor and members of minority groups. (Brennan and Nelson, 1981) The shift in the makeup of the student body came about because the colleges, either by choice in an age of declining admissions or by external decree from various legislative bodies, took on the task of "salvaging" students, rather than simply teaching them. (Cohen and Brawer, 1982)

Academic faculty who once taught sophomore courses designed for transfer students found themselves involved in developmental education. For a person who once spent his time teaching the complexities of the minor British poets of the seventeenth century to find himself teaching the basic sentence is no small change. It requires an adjustment that many found demoralizing. It can result in the jaded quality described by the History professor.

The changes demanded by a period of rapid change are more easily handled if an infusion of new blood accompanies the modifications, but the period of change that characterized generation four was accompanied by tight economic conditions that restricted new hiring. An aging faculty was forced to cope with rapid, unpredictable alterations in their function, their working conditions, their students, and their environments. Many found the conditions uncomfortable and tried to maintain the more comfortable status quo.

Teachers are often resistant to change and are conservative in their practices. Deegan and Tillery (1985) state that, within the profession, several preconditions for conservatism can be found. The authors claim that the teacher's intellectual and emotional investments can, in themselves, be a source of resistance to change. Becoming an expert, either in a subject area or in the art of teaching, is no easy task. It requires a period of years and a lot of effort. To be asked to change can be viewed as the undermining of those years of effort. It is akin to being asked to throw over a lifetime's work.

To affect a change of the magnitude the system demanded is to literally ask a person who has spent his adult life becoming the person he is to become someone else. No one throws over his identity easily, especially when a natural hardening of the professional arteries and a certain level of conservatism has set in.

The sources of the change are also a major factor in the demoralization of the professorate. For the academic faculty, those changes originated from outside; most of the time, they were imposed upon the faculty without the benefit of teacher input or consultation.

Few academic professors made a conscious decision to change: that decision was made for them by a large variety of factors that they perceived as being beyond their control. They came from society at large, from the different categories of students the colleges were recruiting, and from the alteration in the mission of the colleges. The new direction was presented to them by their administrations in a top-down fashion. A change in the nature of the system forced an adaptation upon them.

Since faculty members had no control over these changes, it was only logical that they resist them. It was as though a person became a CPA and found herself counting pebbles for a living. Not only was she expected to count pebbles, her administration told her that counting pebbles was a good thing.

To row against the current is difficult; to work in a system one feels has gone wrong, while feeling helpless to correct the drift creates a sense of powerlessness.

Seidman (1985) also noted this loss of power and attributes it to a growing anti-intellectualism on community college campuses. For a researcher to suggest that an institution of higher learning has created a climate where anti-intellectualism flourishes is a harsh statement. Where does this climate come from? According to Seidman, the loss of intellectual fervor is a result of the fact that the community college has "taken on an easy skepticism about intellectual work; in its divorce of research from teaching and its attempt to reach the 'nontraditional' student, the community college has separated action, teaching and intellect." (p. 263)

An alteration in the goals of the system, therefore, has created an unanticipated side effect. Seeing true and deep commitment to an intellectual purpose fading, faculty and administration reacted by adopting skepticism about the system's intellectual underpinnings. One effect of the development of the comprehensive community college that few could have foreseen, then, was the loss of intellectual rigor. Spread thin, the institution lost its intellectual bearings. Like a spurned lover claiming he didn't really value the woman who rejected him anyway, the colleges, to cover the pain of the loss, took on an aura of anti-intellectualism.

Academic faculty value the life of the intellect; they entered a system which also valued it in order to exercise the life and to help develop that same value in others. To be unable, because of systemic reasons beyond their control, to touch the quality they value most inevitably creates a feeling of powerlessness.

This sensation of powerless in the faculty intensified during the fourth generation but it is actually no new thing. In truth, the systemic nature of the community colleges planted the seeds of anti-intellectualism as far back as the early sixties. In 1967, Garrison reported it in faculty who were dismayed at their inability to set standards for the type of students they worked with, as well as the time it took to reach the increased numbers of students.

Further studies over the years indicate that the feeling has simply grown stronger. It is no longer attributable only to the type of students. Now other conditions, such as the structure, bureaucracy and layers of authority in their institution contribute to a lack of perceived power. (Cohen, 1987)

We will speak more about this feeling of helplessness when we discuss the conditions that members of the adjunct faculty face daily. For the moment, let it suffice to say to say that the possibly unhealthy nature of the changes that the system has undergone has created a feeling of powerlessness in one of the groups that most directly effects the success or failure of students.

The colleges will feel the effects for a long time to come.

Chapter 5:

Adjunct Faculty

Before discussing adjunct faculty, let us profile two members of that group:

Marie. Marie is a 46 year old married woman who has been teaching in an adjunct capacity for sixteen years. Currently, she holds positions at a suburban community college and at a branch of the state university. She describes herself as discontented with her status as an adjunct. "My attitude's changed," she says. "Sixteen years ago, I got my master's and wanted more in my life, so I applied here [at the community college] and got on as an adjunct. I had thoughts similar to a full-time professional. Back then, teaching was something extra and I was happy at first. That happiness lasted a few years."

When her children were older she was in a position to work full-time and wanted to practice her profession on that basis. That desire brought an end to her happiness. "Adjuncting was a disservice to myself. There were no benefits, no retirement, and I was in a position to want those things, so I tried to make the switch. Two full-time positions opened in those early years and I applied for both of them. Both times I got turned down. All my qualifications, all of my service, was overlooked. I lost both jobs."

This began a pattern that continued. "A couple of years ago, they opened up two more full-time positions. I applied and got turned down again. The Division chair, the adjunct coordinator and the department chair met with me and said I didn't seem to be available, so I must not be really interested."

Marie bristles at the memory. "There's a real catch-22 at work here. To be marketable, I have to be here, but I work on two campuses so I can't be here. It's a problem for them. Well, it's a problem for me, too. Working two campuses is a hassle. I have to juggle classes, meetings, all of it. If I'm given a class at the other campus and they call and offer me one here at the same time, I have to turn it down because I'm already committed. Then they say I'm not interested because I turned down the class. They hold it against me."

"They owe me," She says vigorously, "My student evaluations are high, I've been observed, I've been given teaching level advancements, I've given them sixteen years of service. I should be given a full-time job. There's a responsibility on their part. But it's not going to happen."

But she also holds herself partially responsible. "I haven't done any career building, but there's nothing I could do about that. I was working and raising my kid. I've got no work beyond the master's," She says resignedly. "My credentials are as good as most of the full-timers' around here, but they keep raising the ante, demanding more. So if some hotshot fresh out of grad school comes along, he's going to be given the job over me."

"There's no integrity in this place," she says flatly. "They make efforts to keep me informed about job openings and all, but they don't mean it. There are mixed emotions on their part. Maybe some guilt. It's just not fair."

Marie does not simply feel that her community college has treated her unfairly by not giving her full-time work. Her sense of a lack of fairness goes further than that. She feels excluded from the daily life of the division. "I want to know what's going on in the department. You overhear full-time faculty talking about stuff and you're never really sure what they're talking about. You're provided minutes of meetings, sure, but you don't get a context so you don't really know what's happening, what it all adds up to. There's a Catch-22 at work here: they'll invite you to meetings, but they know you can't come. But it isn't just the meetings. It's the small stuff. Even when it comes to giving gifts to secretaries and all, you're left out. Nobody comes to you. You feel excluded."

Because of her perception of the lack of fairness and her accompanying perception of exclusion, Marie reports that even though she might have the opportunity to participate in the affairs of the division, she would choose not to exercise it. Whatever energies she devotes to the job, she will devote to the university where she also does part-time teaching, the institution she feels has treated her better. "The school gives me a desk and space in an office. You have to have an office to meet student needs. Over there, I get paid $1750 per course, as opposed to twelve-five here. Also, if I do extra work, I get paid for it. The students are generally easier to teach. Here, I deal with lower level abilities. People can only excel to their limitations and the students here are limited. The university lets me teach juniors and seniors."

She shakes her head angrily and repeats, for emphasis: "There's just no integrity here."

Discussion. Although Marie characterizes herself as discontented, a deep bitterness comes through in her behavior and language. She stares defiantly at a partner in conversation as though daring him to disagree with her, as if waiting to be challenged. When she speaks, she nods her head vigorously, agreeing behaviorally with her own words, emphasizing them; if no one else agrees with her interpretation of events, her attitude says, it does not matter: her own sense of certainty is strong enough to compensate. Her behavior, though, indicates that she does not anticipate that others will be as certain as she is.

Her experiences have disillusioned her. She is a veteran teacher whose professional life has not worked out as she expected. Now, in midcareer, she has no more illusions; they have been replaced by bitterness. Losing the two full-time jobs early in her career affected her strongly. She viewed the move from adjunct to full-time as a natural progression, a step that would be ready for her when she decided it was time to make it. When it didn't work out that way, she took the rejection personally and became bitter.

Even though she verbalizes a partial self responsibility, Marie demonstrates a victim's mentality. She has been wronged, she believes, so often and so completely that it is almost as though a vendetta existed against her. As a result, helplessness, a sense of having no hope, has set in.

She describes the administration of the division as holding grudges against her, having a responsibility to her that is not being fulfilled, lacking integrity, behaving in a two-faced fashion when they try to keep her informed of career advancement possibilities, and excluding her. Both their actions and motives are, in her mind, suspect. Her speech suggests that she sees herself as the wronged innocent victim of some power elite who have it in for her for no good reason; they owe her but will neither pay her nor acknowledge the debt.

Marie admits she gives nothing but is still angered when she gets nothing in return. She readily acknowledges that her loyalty is to another institution but is still angered because this one does not give her the loyalty to which she believes she is entitled.

She perceives nothing to be her fault. Even her lack of career building, the single area she accepts partial responsibility for, is excused by the fact that she was helpless; she had to work and raise her child. The notion that all of one's problems are the fault of someone else, that one is owed and not paid, that one gives and gets nothing in return because the gifts are not appreciated, and that consequently one is entitled but does not receive that entitlement is the attitude of a powerless, betrayed victim. Such an attitude exists within Marie's mind.

Terry. A thirty-two year old male PHD candidate, Terry has been teaching in an adjunct capacity for six years, while searching for a full-time job. Currently, he teaches six courses at two separate community colleges. He describes his situation as unique in that he isn't simply seeking a full-time job; he wants the right position. "I'm in a position to be selective," he explains, "because my wife is a professional and we have benefits.

"A lot of adjuncts don't and benefits would be terrific for them, a tremendous help. I think they ought to offer some kind of fringe benefits, even on a pro rata basis. For me, it doesn't matter because I have my wife's help anyway, but I'm sure it would be tremendously helpful to others. It's a crucial reason some people drop out of the profession."

Terry describes his professional life as stressful. "Teaching at two different schools is a lot of work. What makes it more so is I drive all over hell's half acre. The time I have off that I could spend preparing, I spend driving. I find myself on the road all the time. Right now I commute between eighty miles per day.

"There's a lot of stress. Mondays and Wednesdays I have a twelve and one o'clock class at one college and then I have fifty minutes to get to the other campus. I've gotten kind of used to it, though. I can't worry about whether I'm going to get there on time or not. I tell my students if I'm a little late, hang in there, I'll be there."

Travel has been the major motif of his working life. He has taught simultaneously at more than one institution for most of his career and always scampered from college to college. Although he accepts it as part of the profession -- "It's always been that way for adjuncts" -- he has decided to narrow his field and deliberately restrict his commute to the current one. "I'm pretty much guaranteed adjunct work at these two schools now, so I can exercise some degree of control."

Still the commute affects the job. Office hours are a problem. "They have to be sparse. The one place I get marked down on student evaluation is the question of whether or not I'm available out of class. Nobody holds it against me, neither students nor other people in the department, but it happens. I'm forced to do the minimum, that would be an hour a week. That's about all I can do. I compensate by giving students my home phone number. Sure, I'd rather deal with it at the office, but if you don't have an office...." He shrugs, his voice trailing off.

Terry views adjunct work as a mixed blessing, a way of doing the teaching he loves, but one that has a high cost attached to it. In the recent past, he has been a finalist for three full-time jobs, but has not been offered one. "In two of the jobs I was a finalist for, doing adjunct teaching definitely hurt me because they told me they wanted to see that I'd held at least a one year contract instead of piecemeal work every semester. It seems to be kind of a theme; I've been rejected because I work part-time instead of temporary full-time.

"Being an adjunct can look bad on paper. There is some kind of stigma. It can work against you another way also. If you succeed at adjunct teaching, it creates a situation that might be untenable. I'm up for an instructor position at another community college. I'm already an assistant professor at one college and an associate professor here on an adjunct level, so I don't know if I could take that position. On paper, it would look like a demotion and could create problems for me down the line. Most adjuncts, though, have no position to negotiate from. They're so desperate they'll take whatever's available."

He also attributes his difficulty in finding full-time work to his own selectivity. "My perception of the academic world right now is they'd like you to take these one year positions, instead of worrying about the equity in your home, moving your kids around and so forth. My wife has her career, the equity in my home is going up at an incredible rate and my kids are happy, so I can't afford to move for a one year job. I like this area. I'm willing to move, but only in the right circumstances. About this time every year, I go through the application process and it really disturbs your life. Sure, I'll have my life disturbed, but only on my terms. So if my teaching situation is less than ideal right now, I have to take responsibility for that. I make my choices and take the consequences.

You have to look at a whole life, not just a job."

When he looks at the job, however, Terry sees several areas in which it could be improved. Jokingly, he says, "Well, they could improve it really quickly by making me full-time." Turning serious, he adds, "One way they could improve it for everybody is to simply admit that being paid less for the same job is wrong. But if the adjunct is willing.... Why don't they let me do more with my classes and pay me more? There's no excuse for it. There's a double penalty for adjuncts; they penalize you by not paying you enough and they do it again by allowing you to work under inadequate conditions. If they do that, the quality of your performance has to suffer."

Terry carefully points out that he is complaining about the situation of adjuncts in general, not just his own. "I was brought in pretty high on the salary scale, based on some stuff I'd done in graduate school. They even counted my TA work as experience. They could have bought me cheaper. After three years, I was promoted to associate adjunct, so as far as treatment goes, I don't feel I've been treated badly. I don't believe I'm looked down on by anyone -- full-timers, administrators, or students.

"Still, adjunct work is exploitive. I notice there's many more women than men doing it and I can't help but wonder if they can afford to be adjuncts because their husbands work. And I can't help but wonder if that's a part of administrative thinking."

The exploitation theme is central to his thinking. "This college, all colleges, exploit the part-time labor force. We at the community college are supposed to be the trend setters, the fresh thinkers, but we're just playing the same old game, exploiting an underclass."

He sees two issues working against a solution to the exploitation problem: economics and fairness. Bringing everyone on full-time, he recognized, was simply not feasible; "It would raise the cost of education, put it out of reach of the people who need it most. Community colleges would cost as much as universities." Still, exploitation could not be excused as an economic necessity. "I think you have to put some kind of cap on it. If the work is there for, say, arbitrarily, three years, they should be obligated to create a position. After they've exploited you for three years, they've kept the cost down. At that time, they should, at the very least, give you a one year contract."

Discussion. Terry's behavior and language differ significantly from Marie's. He is relaxed in an interview, smiling quickly and easily, meeting the gaze of an interviewer, and offering occasional jokes.

Though he describes himself as aggressive, there is no aggression in his manner.

Because he has a cushion -- his wife's job -- he is able to view his own work situation with a degree of detachment that is lacking in the other people profiled. He offers a different perspective: that of a person who has made his choices, is aware that he has made them, and is able to live reasonably comfortably with the consequences of those choices. Terry accepts the stress of traveling teaching and accommodates it because he sees his own responsibility for his situation. He has made moves to control the stress, such as limiting his teaching -- and therefore his sources of income -- to two colleges. He is also able to control the stress because of his perspective; Terry sees teaching as part of an overall life, rather than all of it; teaching is a spoke, not the bicycle.

Although he has not connected with a full-time job, he has made a success of adjunct teaching. He regularly gets the maximum number of sections available and his contributions have been recognized by raises and promotions at both of his host colleges. Terry attributes this success to his aggression. He does not wait to accept whatever offer is forthcoming, but actively tries to construct a place for himself; He scans the catalog for courses no longer offered and asks for a chance to reactivate them, for example.

Terry, then, has created a position for himself, instead of waiting for one to be created.

Perhaps the security gained by this self-creation is the reason he, unlike Marie, speaks to the conditions of adjuncts in general. He is careful to except himself when he speaks of the need for benefits and one-year contracts, reminding listeners that he has his wife's benefits and will not accept a one-year contract. He speaks of what is needed for the profession, rather than himself individually. If the adjunct faculty is a herd, he is one of it, but does not see his role as simply grazing.

Even though he recognizes that adjunct work is exploitive, he is able to recognize the need for the institution to engage in a certain degree of exploitation; without it, he points out, the cost of education would be prohibitively expensive. He seeks a negotiated end to the practice, after a given period of time, implying that the institution has an obligation to those it exploits, an implied contract of sorts.

One cannot say if Terry's situation is truly unique; a great many adjunct faculty members, male and female, are advantaged by having a mate's benefits and live contentedly in homes with growing equity. Terry's perception of himself as unique, however, has enabled him to make moves toward becoming the master of his fate, rather than the powerless victim that Marie presents.

Adjunct Teaching and Personal Power. If full-time faculty are becoming disenchanted with their working conditions and are experiencing a loss of power, imagine what the situation must be for adjuncts. They are the Cinderellas of the community colleges, the less valued step-sisters who are taken for granted, given the responsibility for the dirty work and never invited to the glitzy parties. They are the part-time workers with no benefits, low pay and undesirable shift assignments that Wal-Mart hires to supplement their full-time workers. In most community colleges, as in most Wal-Marts, there are more part-timers than full-timers.

Among the changes higher education has witnessed over the last two decades is a dramatic increase in the use of adjunct faculty. During the seventies, the use of full-time faculty grew nine percent, while the use of adjuncts increased fifty percent (AAUP, 1981).

The early eighties saw a further increase. According to the National Center for Educational Statistics (Fox, 1984), the use of part-time faculty increased eighty percent over a four year period, while the use of full-time faculty rose only eleven percent. The pattern of reliance on part-time faculty shows no sign of abating.

Across the nation, the faculty of two-year colleges has become dominated by adjuncts; more than fifty percent of community college teachers are now part-timers. Most of these institutions now hire more part-timers than they do full-time instructors; adjuncts outnumber regular faculty.

The main reason is economic. As financial resources shrank, the use of part-timers expanded. Academic administrators, faced with the problem of delivering quality instruction to students at a time when changing political priorities made fewer dollars for faculty available, viewed the hiring of part-timers as an attractive move. The attraction is simple to understand; typically, part-timers in community colleges are compensated at a low rate and receive no fringe benefits, such as hospitalization or dental insurance, retirement or tuition reimbursement. In addition, they are provided with few, if any, support services. Leslie (1982) reports watching adjuncts conduct conferences with students in crowded stairwells because no offices were available for their use.

In some cases, the increase in the use of adjuncts is indirectly, rather than directly, due to financial shortages. Colleges facing good times also rely on adjuncts. Tuchman (1981) reports that administrators at schools experiencing temporary enrollment surges hire part-timers because they do not wish to offer tenure to faculty. They fear they may have to deal with a surplus when the surge ends. "The presence of a pool of gypsy faculty provides the flexibility to fill crowded classrooms today without the risk of having a surplus of faculty in the future." (p. 9)

Although they might use adjuncts heavily, many school administrations inadvertently neglect the overall welfare of part-time faculty members because they perceive the individual member's needs to be different from their own; they accept the standard myth of adjunct faculty, which says that the adjunct is a professional who has full-time employment elsewhere, a Certified Public Accountant, for example, who stops by the institution on his way home to teach a course in accounting and is rewarded by receiving the prestige of being associated with an institution of higher learning.

It is true that in certain departments, such as business, which rely heavily on the use of part-timers, many individual teachers do have full-time jobs elsewhere; however, the standard myth does not hold up when applied to the Humanities. In that field, more than sixty percent of part-timers have no other source of income; most teach part-time while searching for a full-time teaching position. (Gappa, 1984, p. 29) The needs of part-timers in the Humanities, therefore, differ from those suggested by the standard myth.

Regardless of needs and standard myths, the Carnegie Foundation for the Advancement of Teaching views the trend toward increasing use of adjuncts with alarm:

> Part-time faculty operate under unfavorable conditions: no offices, lack of time on campus, usually hired on short-term contracts. Because of a fragmented schedule, it is difficult for them to develop deep institutional commitments and their connections with other faculty and students are tenuous at best. The spirit of community is weakened. (Boyar, 1987, p. 137)

For these reasons, the Foundation recommends that no more than twenty percent of the undergraduate faculty be made up of part-timers. The commission further suggests that it is essential that their employment be educationally justified. Community colleges routinely violate this recommendation.

For a combination of reasons, many related to economic factors, others based on specific educational needs, the use of adjunct faculty in the community colleges is not going to decrease. If the concern stated by the

Carnegie Foundation is justified, a problem could result. As the report of the Foundation states, quality of instruction could suffer and the spirit of community could be weakened.

This degeneration of instruction and community could happen because of the role many adjuncts find thrust upon them: "stepchildren of the institution." (McGuire, 1984) Poorly paid, with little or no fringe benefits, little or no institutional or Divisional support, little or no staff development training, and a tenuous connection to the school that employs her, the adjunct often feels she is left to fend for herself, Cinderella left to clean the chimney while her sisters go to the ball.

How accurate is this perception? A study by McClelland (1981) suggests it is accurate indeed. McClelland surveyed the membership of the Council of Writing Program Administrators, a prime source of data since writing programs use many adjuncts. The results showed what some researchers would consider an administrative lack of concern with the question of adjunct faculty.

Many administrators could not complete the survey because they did not keep detailed and accurate records on the use of adjuncts. The thirty-nine percent who were able to respond, however, painted a picture that, from the point of view of an adjunct, can be considered bleak. Only twenty-four percent of part-time faculty members received any kind of fringe benefits; Of the responding schools, only twenty-five percent assigned academic rank to adjuncts. Seventy-five percent of the schools paid less than $400 per semester hour: If a full-time faculty member were paid at that rate for teaching four three hour courses per semester, his or her salary would be $9600 for the academic year. Few adjuncts, however, approached that figure; only twenty percent of the responding institutions allowed them to teach four courses per semester.

Not only are adjuncts not rewarded to the extent that full-timers are, they also lack a crucial element in the full-time faculty member's academic life: the ability to plan their work schedules and their courses. An administrator explained that most part-timers are hired at the last minute, sometimes on the day they begin teaching. It is not unusual, he said, for him to be on the phone searching for adjuncts to cover unassigned classes on the first day of a new term.

Teachers confirm this hiring pattern. One community college adjunct reported, "For seventeen years I have worked never knowing whether I had a job or not until the day or so before classes started. I wish there were a better way to arrange things." (Yang & Zak, 1981. p.101-02)

A New York adjunct described his experience with the instability of the field this way:

> Fall semester I worked at two schools. In November, one of those schools told me I was among the lucky ones who would be rehired in the spring. I would teach two three-hour classes. During intercession, I planned the classes, chose texts, and got thoroughly excited about meeting my new students. Four days before the new term began, the other school offered me two four-hour classes. Although the extra two hours would have meant more money, I decided to stick with the first school, where I had really enjoyed the creative atmosphere and the interaction between adjuncts and full-timers. The day before classes began, I received a phone call saying that due to low registration, my six hours had been cancelled. The caller's warmth and words of sympathy helped little. I quickly called the second school, but, of course, the two classes they'd offered me were already covered (Blank and Greenberg, 1981, p.10).

Although most administrations are sympathetic, some offer an odd justification for their treatment of adjuncts. The part-timers, they say, are beginning teachers who lack experience and must, like most entry-level employees in any field, expect a touch of difficulty at the start of their career. Some administrators even glamorize the adjunct's situation; Wallace (1984) reports that an English department chair from a college in New York City justified the adjunct situation there by claiming it to be "a kind of exotic graduate assistantship before PH.D.'s moved on to their real jobs in a year or two." (p. 7) Wallace comments: "His analysis of the situation overlooked the fact that, after five or six years, most of these part-time faculty in New York have discovered that their unstable teaching assignments are as close as they'll ever come to full-time teaching jobs." (p. 7-8)

The New York administrator's analysis also overlooks the fact that most adjuncts are not beginners. Indeed, an Ohio study (Yang and Zak, 1981) shows they are very well professionally developed and equally well experienced. Approximately 25% of all part-timers held doctorates (or the highest professional degree in their fields) The average adjunct had two years of full time teaching experience and four years of part-time experience. 112 members of the sample of 1,514 had published one or two books, 12 had issued three or four books and thirteen had published five or more; about 30% had published one or more articles and 35% had presented papers at professional meetings. Clearly these are not people who had moved along to their "real jobs" in a year or two.

To reiterate, for most adjuncts, such as those working in the Humanities, a field that routinely uses large amounts of part-timers, (Wallace, 1984) the standard myths about adjuncts do not hold up; most teach part-time while actively searching for full-time employment and have no other source of income.

The systemic nature of the problem. The problems adjuncts must live with come from the systemic nature of the schools. Every system develops its own paradigm, its own way of perceiving and interpreting reality. Those paradigms are accepted by the people within the system. The result is that the college as a whole adopts a comprehensive and agreed-upon world view.

The economic downturn of the eighties caused the student population of the community colleges to swell. Students flocked back to school in an effort to beat the recession, causing a systems push. The colleges, caught in an unexpected squeeze - an increasing student population during a time of economic belt-tightening - responded by hiring adjunct faculty, gypsy scholars who worked part-time, were paid by the course and received no fringe benefits. For politicians and administrators, adjuncts offered the best of two separate worlds; they covered classes while cutting costs.

The move from a reliance on a full-time faculty to a dependence on part-timers represents a dramatic shift in the way the educational mission is perceived and carried out by community colleges - no less than a shift in the educational paradigm - because even though the economic conditions that brought on the increase in adjuncts have eased, their use constitutes a trend that shows little sign of abating.

Adjuncts and the community college mission. Greive (1983) states that one strength of adjunct faculty members is that they are more likely to accept the mission of the community college. Cooke (1972) also found that part-timers were more likely to understand and accept the community college role than full-timers.

If Greive and Cooke are correct, how can we account for the fact that part-time faculty in the Humanities report feeling isolated and estranged? (Wallace, 1984) If people who are committed to a prevailing philosophy are given an opportunity to work in an environment that manifests that philosophy, satisfaction ought to result. Yet it has not. Instead these part-timers report that they feel alone, misunderstood and mistreated by their full-time colleagues. How can this dichotomy be explained?

A possible explanation grows out of Leslie's (1983) research. Since Humanities teachers are described by Leslie as less likely to be completely committed to the prevailing philosophy, they are also likely to perceive of themselves as different from those who do. The difference they feel is likely to manifest itself in the way they treat adjuncts.

Characteristics of Adjunct Faculty. As far back as 1977, Kandzer wrote:

> Over the past decade, the part-time faculty member has become a critical component of the nation's community college system. His emergence has resulted from a number of interrelated factors. Among these are: (1) the nation's economic systems; (2) the rapid and in many instances unpredictable growth of the nation's community college system; (3) the pledge this system has to keep its doors open, to remain flexible and adaptable to the needs of the community it serves; and (4) to continue to serve primarily as an institution of teaching excellence. (78)

Kandzer wrote just before the explosion. By 1980, in over twenty-one states, more than 50% of the faculties of two-year colleges consisted of part-time members (Community and Junior College Directory, 1980). The use of these part-timers had been noticed earlier but had not been considered worth of deep study. Bender and Hammons (1972) stated that "relatively little has been done to study how effectively part-time staff have been used in serving students, and how effectively the institution has been serving them" (p.21).

Sources of part-time faculty. With the increased notice of part-timers came an increased interest in their backgrounds. Lombardi (1975) identified five major sources of part-timers: Day faculty, other colleges, K-12 schools, non-educational fields and recent university graduates. Proportions from each source, however, will vary, according to such factors as educational policy, the location of the college, and the number of overload units the institution permits full-time faculty to teach. Lombardi points out that colleges with large occupational programs rely heavily on business, government and industry, while professional programs, such as medicine and law, recruit working professionals to teach specialized courses.

Other studies agree with Lombardi's conclusion that proportions vary widely. Kennedy (1967) found that in Illinois, 53% of part-time faculty came from the secondary schools, while in Maryland only 26% did. Messerschmidt (1967) discovered that virtually all adjuncts in Michigan came from business and industry. In North Carolina (Cooke, 1972) 29.8% have their origins in education, 28.8% come from business, while 19% were otherwise unemployed homemakers. In California, most adjuncts are full-time day faculty teaching overloads (Ross, 1975).

Academic Preparation. In the seventies, a number of studies undertook to discover if a discrepancy existed between the academic preparation of part-timers and their full-time counterparts. Waddell (1978) reported that in Arizona, the part-time faculty of urban two-year colleges had better credentials than adjuncts at rural two-year colleges: 61.9% of the urban group held Master's degrees, as opposed to 41.6% at rural colleges. Doctorates were held by 7.9% of the urban group, while only 5.4% of the rural group held these degrees.

As a general conclusion, the work of Lombardi (1975), Seitz (1971), and Kennedy (1967) indicates that part-timers have earned fewer graduate degrees and have less teaching experience than full-timers. This fact can be explained by the fact that many adjuncts teach in vocational programs or in credit-free programs where credentials are not essential.

When Humanities divisions are examined, the discrepancy between full- and part-timers disappears. In a nationwide study of Humanities faculty, Cohen (1975) found that full-timers held more advanced degrees than part-timers but only by 3%. More recently, Wallace (1984) has confirmed Cohen's findings.

Effectiveness of part-time teachers. The work of Kraus (1962) Kandzer (1977) and Cagle (1978) declares that few differences between full-time and part-time teachers exist in regard to quality. Friedlander (1979) drew an entirely different picture, however.

Freidlander asked how part-timers differed from full-timers and discovered that the differences were profound, touching almost every variable studied. He found that part-timers had less teaching experience, both in total and at their current institution, and held fewer academic credentials. They had less input into the selection of materials to be used in their courses, assigned fewer pages to read, used less instructional media, recommended or required students to attend fewer out-of-class activities, and placed less emphasis on written assignments in determining grades.

Adjuncts also demonstrated less awareness either of their particular campus or their field. They were less aware of campus activities and were less likely to have access to or to use instructional support services. In terms of professional development, they read fewer journals, were less likely to be members of professional organizations, and attended fewer meetings and conferences. They were also less likely to request released time to develop courses or to participate in professional development activities.

Freidlander also claimed adjuncts were less likely to hold office hours, serve on committees, or to work with other instructors, administrators, and support service personnel. For these reasons, he concluded, "the quality of instruction provided by an institution is likely to be adversely affected as the number of faculty employed as part-time increases" (p. 13).

The differences Freidlander points to with alarm are the same ones adjuncts complain about; confronted with the Friedlander's list, many adjuncts responded that they wished to do these things, but their situations, the conditions under which they work, and the institutions at which they work, would not permit them.

Taxonomies of adjunct faculty. Although these studies discuss adjuncts as a group, it is important to recognize that part-time faculty members do not fall easily into a single pattern; they are as unique and distinct as any collection of individuals.

The taxonomy of part-timers constructed by Biles and Tuchman (1986) demonstrates the futility of trying to assemble personal statistics. Their taxonomy identifies seven categories of part-time faculty, along with the percentages of adjuncts nationally falling into each category:

1. The semi-retired: Ex-full-time academics who scale down their activities to a part-time basis; ex-full-timers outside of academe who are semi-retired; semi-retired who have taught full-time throughout their entire careers. (2.8%)

2. Students: Employed as part-timers in institutions other than the one at which they hope to receive a degree. (21.2%)

3. Hopeful full-timers: Those with no prior experience in academe who are working part-time to become full-time, and those with prior experience working part-time because they cannot find a full-time position. (16.6%)

4. Full-mooners: Those who hold another job of 35 or more hours per week. (27.6%)

5. Part-mooners: Those with two or more part-time jobs of less than 35 hours per week. (13.6%)

6. Homeworkers: Those who work part-time primarily to care for children and other relatives. (6.4%)

7. Part-unknowners: Those whose reasons for becoming part-time are unknown. (11.8%)

These categories show that adjuncts range in age from students to retirees, indicating that their level of experience will range as widely as their ages do. The taxonomy also suggests that part-timers have a wide variety of reasons for being part-time employees. Generalizations about adjuncts, then, should be made cautiously. It should also be noted that this taxonomy was constructed in 1976, before the budget crunches of the eighties; reasons and motivations of part-timers may have changed since then.

The taxonomy of Biles and Tuchman classifies by motivation. Tobias (in Biles and Tuchman, 1983) has developed one that classifies by employment situation:

1. Moonlighters: Persons who are employed in another job, but teach one course. They have no fringe benefits, no tenure or sabbatical accrual, no advisees or committee work, or a departmental vote.

2. Twilighters: Persons who are not otherwise employed, but whom the institution chooses not to give a regular part-time faculty position. They have no departmental vote but receive prorated fringe benefits and have longer contracts.

3. Sunlighters: Regular faculty appointments and like regular full-time faculty in every way except the amount of time they work. They receive pro-rated fringe benefits, committee assignments, and advisees and are eligible for tenure and sabbatical accrual. Their probation period is no longer than seventeen semesters and they have an opportunity to negotiate full-time faculty status at a later date.

4. Persons on occasional part-time leave: Those whose regular full-time faculty appointment is retained and whose probationary period is extended proportionately. They may extend their part-time leave or return to full-time status at any time. This category of part-time faculty is not restricted to women who have small children, although the expectation is that such people will use it most.

Although Tobias classifies by employment situation, a growing body of research indicates that in the Humanities, at least, her classifications are not largely not relevant because of changes in the operational situations in which many colleges find themselves. MacGuire (1986) states that because part-time faculty accrue costs for the hiring institution of only one/third those of regular faculty, and because many colleges anticipate a steadily declining population over the next dozen years, "many who aspired to join the ranks of full-time college professors . . . no longer to see that choice as viable." (p. 27) This, of course, means that the taxonomies' categories will shift as people find themselves forced into categories of lesser desirability that they would not have chosen for themselves.

It must also be considered that Biles and Tobias were at the time of their studies administrators. When scholars who teach in the Humanities examine the issue of the use of adjunct faculty, they often paint a picture that is radically different. Wallace (1984) offers a taxonomy that states there are only three legitimate uses of part-time faculty:

1. Moonlighters from another field who bring to the institution a special expertise that it couldn't afford otherwise.

2. Regular part-timers who have prepared for and planned lifelong careers in college teaching in their chosen fields (corresponds to Tobias' Sunlighters).

3. Paraprofessionals who have prepared themselves by a combination of education and teaching experience for a lifelong career in teaching crucial language arts skills to undergraduates (corresponds to Tobias' Twilighters).

People in two out of three of the categories in Wallace's taxonomy have prepared for lifelong careers in teaching, indicating a desire for full-time employment. Biles and Tuchman and Tobias, on the other hand, have many more categories for part-timers who desire and are satisfied with part-time employment.

Degree of satisfaction. Studies indicate that most adjuncts are not satisfied with part-time employment. As stated previously, more than sixty percent teach part-time while searching for full-time employment. Regular faculty positions are not often forthcoming, however. The "Modern Language Association Statement on Part-time Faculty" (1982) might inadvertently point to a reason many adjuncts find it difficult to move into a full-time position when it speaks of the part-timers' "limited commitment" and "low professional standing."

Many adjuncts find that, when applying for full-time work, their experience as part-timers actually works against them. Kantrowitz (1981) states that her applications for full-time status at her college were never seriously considered because she had taught part-time, even though her credentials were equal to or better than those of competing candidates. Neither her publication record nor her service as an expert reader for PMLA was enough to overcome the "stigma of having taught part-time." (37)

Kantrowitz's experience is not atypical. Wallace (1984) reports a reluctance of institutions to hire adjuncts for full-time work and states that many institutions are skeptical about the part-timers they hire; one administrator in Wallace's study claimed they exploit the institutions that hire them.

Conditions of Adjunct Employment. The conditions under which most adjuncts are hired and work explain both their dissatisfaction and the stigma that sometimes attaches to adjuncts. Usually, adjuncts receive only cursory interviews and appointment procedures. One administrator explained that superficial nature of the interview process in this way: "Classes started today and I have six uncovered sections. I don't have time to go into detail. I have to take whoever I can get." Research, creativity and even previous service to the institution are rarely considered in adjunct appointments. The "stepchildren of the institution" perception results from these procedures. Most colleges leave the hiring of adjuncts to department or division heads. Therefore, only a single person reviews the credentials and interviews adjuncts. Since hiring is done primarily from a local pool of talent, jobs are often not advertised. "I can't advertise jobs," one department head stated. "Until final figures are in, I don't know if they're going to exist." Hiring is done from personal contacts.

Part-timers work under extraordinary circumstances; they do not know what they will teach, when they will teach it, where they will teach it, what texts they will use, or even if they will teach, until the last minute. These conditions, of course, can create an underdog mentality on the part of the adjunct and a perception of lesser value of the part-timer on the part of full-timers and administrators.

The working life of adjunct faculty members can best be characterized by its contradictions. They describe themselves as relatively content, but when offered an opportunity to discuss their situations, they do not describe contentment. Status and respect, they say, are not issues, but they are sorely bothered by their lack of those qualities. They declare that they have sources of support on the job, but their comments indicate that they are not fully confident of the degree or quality of that support. They claim to feel valued, but their discussion does not validate that claim.

Most significantly, they do not feel that anything can be done about their situation; they feel powerless. The president of one community college placed this helplessness in perspective. Noticing that even though the college paid less for adjuncts than the neighboring universities, a need for increased salary was not among the major complaints of the adjuncts, she postulated the possibility that a minority mentality might exist, citing Compton and Galaway's (1984) explanation that a minority mentality is created through interaction with a system: Because the system is so remote and so pervasive, they claim, "Lower-class, minority group individuals cannot be expected to feel that they have a part in the determination of their own destinies in the face of grievances.... (456)

Daily involvement with a social and political system that is stacked against them creates a group of people who have been systematically socialized into apathy and inaction, say the authors.

It must be emphasized that the phrase "minority mentality" is meant to be descriptive rather than judgmental. It must also be emphasized that the authors' discussion would lead to a conclusion that the mentality is a universal response to the conditions described, thereby connoting an inevitability that does not actually exist. No sense of universality or inevitability is merited. The condition is but one of many possible responses. Finally, when applied to adjunct faculty, the term is meant to be metaphorical, not literal. Some might object that it is a metaphor that lacks sensitivity; to a degree, that objection is valid, yet the term, as used, is meant to convey sympathy and understanding. Since the term was used in the literature, it will be used -- with the caveats above -- in this discussion.

Does this minority mentality exist among the part-time faculty in the community college? If previous discussions are accurate, the answer is yes. When adjuncts' discussions are summarized, the following factors become evident:

Adjuncts feel that:
 1: They lack autonomy.
 2: They lack responsibility.
 3: They are not encouraged to participate in decisions that affect their working conditions.
 4: They cannot be involved in the affairs of the division or the college that employs them.
 5: They are not entitled to status or respect.
 6: In the event of a conflict, they will not be backed up by the administration.
 7: They are alienated from the colleges that employ them.
 8: They lack control.
 9: They are powerless.

These factors combine to suggest that a minority mentality does exist and that any effort to integrate adjunct faculty into the colleges more thoroughly must take this mentality into account.

Learned Helplessness. The systemic nature of the community college has created conditions under which both full and part-time faculty are experiencing learned helplessness. Seligman (1975) described learned helplessness as the belief that nothing one does makes a difference. It is the assumption that one cannot have control. As Hooker (1976) says, implicit in the concept of learned helplessness is the assumption that events in life are either controllable or uncontrollable, and that it is a person's experience with these events which shape the belief in his own adequacy. The community college faculty members' experiences with the events and conditions of their work have created a sense of learned helplessness.

How can a group of professionals actively working in their profession demonstrate an assumption that the events of their professional life are beyond their control? How can they, as a result, allow their sense of adequacy to suffer? To understand, we must briefly examine the relationship between people and their work.

Havighurst (1968) points out that there is an interaction between values, attitudes and careers. People tend to choose careers that match their values and attitudes. Teachers, for example, are attracted to the occupation because they want to help young people develop. A wish to help, however, is not the only reason people enter this profession; any occupation, Havighurst adds, can be seen as a complex social role, a set of behaviors, skills, and attitudes that people expect to find in that role. This social role varies from occupation to occupation. A blue collar worker expects to be treated in an authoritarian manner by his foremen; this is simply part of the social role. Members of a college faculty, on the other hand, expect to have "easy, informal, and democratic relations among deans, chairpersons, and teachers." (p. 772) In the community college, those relations have become strained; more and more faculty are reporting distrust and tension between themselves and their administrators and boards.

People also have other expectations for their careers. If these expectations are not met, learned helplessness can result. Miller and Form (1951), taking work histories from groups in Ohio, identified four types of career patterns:

1: The Conventional Career Pattern. The sequence of jobs follows the typical course from initial through trial to stable employment. This is fairly typical of managerial, skilled, and clerical workers.

2: The Stable Career Pattern. In this category are most professional careers, many managers, some skilled, semiskilled and clerical workers. They have gone directly from school or college into the work they now follow.

3: The Unstable Career Pattern. The sequence is trial-stable-trial. The worker may not stabilize his career. This is most frequently seen in semiskilled, clerical, and domestic workers.

4: The Multiple Career Pattern. This involves frequent job changes, with no one type dominant or prolonged. This is observed most frequently in domestic, clerical, and semi-skilled workers.

The researchers found that seventy-three percent of white collar workers had stable or conventional career patterns. Only 46% of blue-collar workers and 29% of unskilled workers had these patterns.

Miller and Form point out that by the time a worker has reached the age of forty-five, she has entered what they call the maintenance stage of a career; she has established herself in a stable career, which she then maintains for some twenty years. She has acquired a family and a position or status in the neighborhood. Her existence is stable and she feels as successful as she ever will.

What would be the result if the worker reached the maintenance stage without having established herself in her career, if she still fell into the unstable career pattern, if she was a professional caught in a pattern characterized by semiskilled, clerical and domestic workers? Certainly this is not the way a person who has undergone graduate education viewed her career possibilities. Yet, the research indicates that more than sixty percent of adjunct faculty members in Humanities Divisions find themselves in exactly this situation. For full-time faculties, many have found that the changing conditions of their work have led to a sort of status demotion; after all their years of teaching, they find themselves doing the work that their University brethren have given over to graduate assistants.

Many of these people have internalized the notion that their career cannot be controlled, that they are and will be unable to practice it the way they intended.

Seligman (1985) researched the parameters of learned helplessness by creating experimental conditions that simulated the different action-outcome contingencies of controllable and uncontrollable events. Subjects who were initially exposed to uncontrollable conditions made progressively fewer responses of any kind -- even under controllable conditions. Instead, after a brief period of "frantic" responding, the subjects gave up and passively endured their situation. Because their experience with trauma occurred first under uncontrollable conditions and because they had learned their responses were of no avail, these subjects gave up; they learned to become helpless.

Given an introduction to their profession under conditions they perceived as uncontrollable -- serving as adjuncts, with no opportunity to exercise the common practices of the full-time faculty, such as control over scheduling, classes taught, office hours and relationships with chairs and other administrators -- these faculty members, once they learned that working as a adjunct was not necessarily a step toward full-time employment, learned to be helpless.

For full-time professors, the situation was similar. In a collegiate atmosphere that once operated on shared governance, collegiality, and a high degree of professional autonomy, these people found that their input was no longer valued and that other people were making their decisions for them without consultation. Schedules, policies and approaches that were once negotiated were declared by fiat. Many faculty, feeling that the revolution was over and they had lost, grew helpless.

It is evident that the current confusion in the community college is both an effect of and a cause of faculty demoralization, passivity and learned helplessness. This is a trend that cannot continue into a fifth generation.

Chapter 6:

The Students

Laura. An eighteen year old graduate of a suburban high school, Laura chose to attend her county's community college because of financial reasons. Her father is an electrician and her mother works as a beautician. "My dad's income varies a lot," Laura says. "When he works, he makes good money, but the industry's up and down, so he's laid off a lot. My mother does pretty well also, but I've got three brothers and sisters, so my parents can't afford to help me. If I want to go to college, it's up to me."

Neither of them went to college; in fact, Laura is the first person in her family go beyond high school. "My brother and my sisters will go. They intend to, but I'm the first. My parents are proud of me, but I think they feel bad at the same time, you know, because they can't give me any help." She doesn't mind. "I always knew that if I wanted to go to college, it was going to be up to me."

The community college makes higher education possible for her. Not only is the tuition within reach, she can continue to live at home while commuting to class. Living about twenty miles from the school, though, causes some problems.

"I have to be here by eight every morning. Even that late, it's hard to get a good parking place. Get here at eight-thirty and you're going to be late for a nine o'clock class because of circling around searching for a spot and the walk from the parking lot."

Her first class, algebra, is at nine. After it, she has a break, so she has breakfast in the cafeteria. While she eats, she generally does her reading for her eleven o'clock Sociology class. After Sociology, she has Creative

Writing, her final class of the day.

"When that one's done, I hit the library and spend a couple of hours working on long range projects. There's no time at night, so I have to get it done then."

When she feels she has put in enough time, Laura goes to the Student Government Association office, where she hangs out with her fellow student leaders or, if one is scheduled, she goes to a club meeting. She is the president of the student drama society and says, "I didn't realize how much time that was going to eat up when I got into it. All the club presidents have the presidents' meetings, sort of a weekly summit conference, then there's the club meetings and the SGA meetings. It goes on forever."

By four in the afternoon, she has wrapped up her extra-curricular responsibilities and heads home to rest for a half an hour or so before she has to go to work. Three evenings a week, she works as a waitress in a family restaurant in a local mall. She works from five until about ten-thirty. "We stop serving at nine-thirty but it takes forever to get out of there."

Her day finally finished, Laura turns down the invitations to go socialize with her friends from the restaurant and heads home to grab some sleep before the next day's classes.

Tuesday and Thursday are light school days. She has chemistry, both class and lab, from nine to ten-fifty. Her acting class follows at eleven. Every other week, she has a private voice lesson at one in the afternoon. She describes Tuesday and Thursday afternoons as a vacation. "I get to go home and sleep, or go to the gym, I can just take it easy. One of my three nights' work is always on the weekend, so I can count on having at least one of the Tuesday or Thursday nights free. I can see my friends, take in a movie, or just read for the next day. I do that a lot because I'm always behind, always behind."

Twice each year, her carefully-planned schedule gets thrown out the window because she is always a part of the student drama production. A promising actor, she is generally cast in the play. If she isn't, she works backstage. "Either way it's six weeks of fourteen hour days, including weekends. I'm lucky, the restaurant is good at letting me off during the run of the plays, but I've still got to keep up with my classes. So, it's six weeks of no sleep time."

Laura feels the sacrifice is definitely worth it, though. "If I didn't do it this way, I'd be working in the restaurant full-time with no hope of going to college or doing anything with my life except serve food. It's hard, but I'm not complaining."

Marco. A young African-American man of twenty, Marco takes four courses at the community college, making sure he carries the twelve credit hours he needs to qualify as a full-time student. Since he does not qualify for student aid - "My mom doesn't make enough money to send me to college but she makes too much for me to get any aid," - there is no particular benefit for Marco in his maintaining full time status, but it is a matter of pride to him. "I've got friends who have been taking classes here for as long as I can remember. They don't get anywhere. That won't happen to me."

Marco schedules all of his classes for the hours between eight and noon. That way he can go directly from work to class. He pulls the overnight shift, from eleven at night until seven in the morning, in the shipping area of a package delivery service. All night he loads trucks. When a truck is full, a driver climbs in and pulls away from the dock and another one takes its place. "All night, there's never a time when there aren't any trucks," he says. "If you don't like hard work, you won't like it here."

When he gets off in the mornings, Marco is tired. "It wears you out, sure, but I don't let it get to me, you know what I mean? I got just about enough time to stop by seven-eleven for a big cup of coffee and make it to my first class." This semester, Marco's third at the college, he is taking courses that do not require many papers: American Civilization, Earth Science, Abnormal Psychology and Introduction to Management. He claims that he does not have time to concentrate on papers and though he knows the avoidance strategy will catch up with him in a later semester, he feels that at this point he has to protect his time.

"I do two classes a day. History and psychology on Monday, Wednesday and Friday, and the others on Tuesday and Thursday. It's the only way I can manage it and, believe me, two classes a day might not sound like much but after you've loaded trucks all night, you're already tired so it'll wear you out. The way it happens is I get off work, stop by for my classes and then head home and go to bed."

He gets about six hours sleep and then gets up, does as much of his school work as he can, spends a little time with his brothers and sisters and then the cycle begins again. "I'm always tired," he says, "I don't think I've gotten enough sleep since I started this college thing."

When asked why he doesn't cut back to part-time work, Marco answers that he can't afford to. "I have to work full-time. I have to pay for my car because if I don't have a car I can't get to work. If I can't get to work, I can't go to school. I've also got to put away money for when I leave the community college and school really gets expensive. One more semester here and I transfer and then my tuition is going to just about triple. I can't afford that and if I don't plan for it right now, I never will be able to pay for it. Then I'll just be one more high school graduate with nothing going for me."

Marco doesn't intend for that to happen. His goal is to make it into management. "I want to work in a coat and tie," he says. He isn't quite sure what field he wants to be a manager in and says that right now it isn't important. "I'd like a job in management here, but I'm not sure that's going to happen. Doesn't matter, though. I'll land somewhere good." Even though he is not sure what field he will enter, Marco is not worried. He will make that decision when the time comes. Right now, he says, all that is important is that he keep his vision focused on a coat and tie. "Management is where it's happening," he says. "The way you can tell how important it is simple; I look around the loading docks at four in the morning and there isn't a single guy in a suit out there. Not one. They're home asleep and they can do that because they got me out here doing the heavy labor."

The community college, Marco says, is his first big step away from heavy labor at four in the morning.

The non-traditional student. As is the case with everything else about the community college, its students, like Laura and Marco, resist all easy generalizations. Perhaps the two most accurate inferences that can be drawn about community college students are that a lot of them exist and that they steadfastly refuse to be easily categorized. As a result of those two inferences, another statement becomes apparent: the fact that the students cannot be easily categorized means that they are the wild card in the system and are rapidly creating a systemic transformation in the two-year college. The colleges are still trying to deal with the new reality these students have brought about, the change from a reasonably conventional, routine and predictable population to the extraordinary one we have today. As a result of the systems push these students are causing, the twenty-first century community college might be radically different from the current one.

As the needs and values of our society change, more people are going to college. They are not simply more of the same people; in recent years, more people who would previously have gone directly into the work force are entering college. The availability and relative lack of expense of the community college is largely responsible for the increase. Indeed, there is a direct connection between the growth of the two-year college and the swelling numbers of college students. The increase in the amount of college students occurred as the numbers of community colleges also swelled.

If you build it, they will come.

Another factor in the increase was the increased availability of financial aid. During the early nineties, a full one/third of community college students received an average of $2000 each in financial aid. Since financial aid is generally designed to assist specific and particular groups who have traditionally been underrepresented, the increase of financial aid not only swelled the numbers but altered the demographics.

Numbers, demographics - everything has changed. In 1960, 500,000 people attended two-year colleges; by the nineties, the figure had swollen to 6 million. Why the astonishing growth? Cohen and Brawer (1996) say it can be attributed to several factors, such as "older students' participation; financial aid; part-time attendance; the reclassification of institutions, the redefinition of students and courses; and high attendance by low-ability, women and minority students." (p. 40-41)

The colleges, according to these authors, also engaged in aggressive recruiting, an activity administrators found natural because "to an institution that tries to offer something for everyone in the community, everyone is potentially a student." (41) A sizeable number of community college students, then, found their way to these schools because the colleges sought out and actively recruited the students the universities did not want. This newer population has been well-studied and the literature groups all of these people into a single category called the *non-traditional student*. The following qualities are ascribed to the category of the non-traditional student:

1: they are older, part-time students whose level of ability might be lower and who are likely to be predominantly female or a member of a minority.

2: Nontraditional students may or may not be interested in acquiring an associate's degree or moving on beyond the two-year diploma.

3: the category generally includes members of the noncredit continuing education courses as well as those enrolled in formal grade-granting classes.

The great growth in the number of these non-traditional students, which led to their becoming the dominant population group on the campuses began with the third generation of institutional history, the rise of the comprehensive community college.

The junior college period was characterized by traditional students, recent high school graduates who preferred to do their freshman and sophomore years' study at the two-year college and then transfer to an upper division school. Indeed, some states, such as Florida, encouraged this academic progression by building a system of junior colleges which were designed to feed graduates into an upper division university created to serve their particular region.

When the junior college evolved into the comprehensive community college, however, the systemic nature of the entire educational enterprise was altered. Now, feeding graduates to upper division schools would be just one of the things the two-year colleges would do and it would not necessarily be the primary focus. The schools would also feed many other types of students - diploma-bearing nontransfer graduates, certificate-holding finishers of special programs, and trained or retrained adults without academic credentials - into the community at large.

Changing definitions of students. For these reasons it is difficult to determine exactly what a student is. Some colleges count virtually anyone who sets foot on campus as a student; to attend a concert or a play, in these administrator's eyes, qualifies one as a student. As community colleges take over programs that were formerly offered by other institutions in the community, such as senior centers or adult education, they tend to count the people in these programs as students, thereby swelling the numbers even more.

The role of a system cannot change without a corresponding change in its vision. As a consequence of this particular alteration of the system's role, the very way the comprehensive community college viewed itself changed. With the change in the way it viewed itself and its mission, the two-year college also changed its methods of accomplishing its revised vision.

In so doing, it also, of course, altered the very notion of what a student was. When the crop of recent high school graduates began drying up due to population shifts, for example, the comprehensive community college looked for a replacement group of tenants. They successfully sought out the underserved older population. Currently the average student is over thirty years old; the mean age is thirty-one.

The newly recruited older students required a different way of doing business. Where the traditional student attends on a full-time basis, the non-traditional one, being older and more established in the society, is much more likely to take classes while holding a job or raising a family; she is likely to attend the main campus at night or to take classes at a satellite branch or a weekend college. Therefore, she is probably a part-time student. This part-time pattern has been the trend for the comprehensive community college, which now has more students taking fewer classes. The major growth since the rise of the comprehensive community college has been in the number of part-time students.

The rise of the nontraditional student makes it more difficult to generalize about students. They come to the campus for too many reasons. The 1986 study by the Center for the Study of Community Colleges discovered that 36% of community college students intended to transfer, while 34% sought job entry skills, 16% were upgrading their skills and 15% attended purely for reasons of personal interest.

Research also indicates that, among non-traditional students, the immediate goal is probably not to transfer to an upper division school. The adult learner is often guided by more pragmatic goals; to upgrade job skills, to fill a resume gap for a promotion or a move to a new and better job, or to simply prepare herself to enter the job market.

Examples of non-traditional students. Robin serves as an example of the non-traditional adult woman student. At the age of thirty-four, she had been with her firm for fifteen years and was holding down a supervisory position in the shipping department on a temporary basis until a new permanent manager could be found. She had been filling the position for a year.

"I was doing a better job than the person who was in that slot before me," she says, "Profits were up, costs were down, morale was high, my evaluations were superb. Everybody agreed I had the job nailed, so I applied for it on a permanent basis."

When she filed her application, Robin discovered she was ineligible to be offered the position she had been successfully holding down on an interim basis. The slot was designated for a person who had credentials in marketing. Robin had no formal knowledge of marketing; although she had been doing marketing on a daily basis as a part of the job and had studied the subject informally, she had no transcript. Her employer told her that before she could be given the job on a permanent basis, she would have to have two years of college with some formal coursework in marketing.

Robin had not felt ready for college when she graduated from high school. "I was a terrible student," she says. "It was hard for me and I was too immature to realize that my lack of interest grew out of fear of failure and poor self-esteem. So I just did what most of the kids I knew did: showed up most days and didn't make trouble. That was the deal, and since I've been back in school, I've learned that people who write about schooling call it the unwritten contract; all you have to do is be there and be quiet and they'll graduate you.

"I did and they did and I went straight into a dead end job. After moving around from bad job to bad job for a few years, I landed at my current company and I liked it. The work is good, the people are too, and I feel valued there. They've given me this chance to get the credentials and are holding the job open instead of passing me over and they're paying for fifty percent of my schooling, so I can't complain."

Robin, then, is a fairly typical adult night student. The need to meet a specific short-term goal brought her to the school and she demanded a pragmatic payoff to her learning, in this case, a promotion. Far more comfortable with the concrete than the abstract, she has little patience with any course that does not directly relate to her need for marketing credentials; she initially resisted and struggled with other required coursework.

Gradually, though, her exposure to learning and her success at it brought about a weakening of her resistance. She is now able to better enjoy her studies and, since she has learned to integrate her coursework into the other areas of her life, she is doing well. She is still guided by the pragmatic principle, however, and has no plans to continue after she finishes her AA program.

Her reluctance to continue is typical of a large group of nontraditional students; driven by specific goals, many simply leave when those goals are met. Others, however, find that the learning experience brings out drives and goals they had not anticipated discovering.

Consider the case of Julie. When she was in high school her record was dismal. "I simply wasn't there," she says, "I had no interest in it at all. I'd be physically in the building, but mentally, I was off in the stars somewhere. I just didn't care."

Music was Julie's life. "After I got into music, my school career got even worse." Her sister was a guitar player, so Julie figured, since her sister had it covered, that the electric guitar, an instrument she loved, was off-limits to her. She took up the electric bass and when she had developed a certain amount of proficiency, she and her sister put a band together. "My future was in rock," she says, "not in the classroom. I wanted to be the next John Entwhistle, the bass player with the Who, and I simply couldn't see beyond that ambition. Even after my sister came to her senses and went off to college, I kept on. The band was working regularly, beginning to make a name for itself, and high school sort of disappeared. I don't recall making a decision to quit; it just happened. I got a GED and bailed."

Julie experienced more success than most musicians. She made a living and was eventually invited to tour the England. While working there, she was invited to join a well-known British band, so she relocated to England where she pursued her career, got married and had a child.

"When Maggie was born, everything changed," Julie says. "Running around a couple of foreign countries playing rock and roll wasn't as much fun anymore, not when I had to leave Maggie behind. I gave it up and we came back to the states."

When Julie was twenty-eight, she entered a community college, unsure of her intentions or her ability. "All I knew was that if I intended to do anything except give bass lessons out of my apartment, I'd need to go to school. At first, all I wanted was to learn some computer skills so I could make a living working in an office somewhere. I'd been doing temp work and at that point,

I just couldn't see beyond office work. I didn't have any academic ambition at all and I was scared to death. School had never been my thing, so going back was really scary."

By the time her freshman year was finished, Julie had a direction. "As unimportant as formal learning had been to me in the old days, as far down the scale of value it was, I was amazed to see that it became the center of my life. I loved college, I loved learning, and suddenly I discovered this love for literature. I wanted to spend the rest of life studying it and teaching it."

Once Julie's goal had surfaced, she pursued it with a total absorption. When the courses she needed weren't available, she talked individual teachers into creating them for her as independent study projects. Originally, by everyone's estimate, including her own, demonstrably one of the lower ability students that Cross refers to, Julie finished community college with a 4.0 average and won a scholarship to study at a state university. She left that school with a Bachelor's degree in Medieval literature and a full scholarship to graduate school, where she is currently finishing her Doctorate work. She has won scholarships to conduct post-doctoral study at Cambridge in England.

The point of Julie's story is obvious: a student who is categorized as nontraditional, who would not be declared "college material" by anyone who judged her by her background, does not necessarily suffer from a lack of ability. One of the great values of the two-year college is that it provides a place where a student can test herself and where a previously underachieving student can, when she is ready, become an achiever.

Julie's experience demonstrates another reason that it is hard to generalize about community college students; since they are embarked on a course of action that causes personal growth, they change rapidly. So do their goals, ambitions and dreams.

Originally brought reluctantly to a community college to pursue a specific short-term goal, Julie's experience was pleasurable enough to bring about a permanent change, which transformed her personally and professionally. Since she views herself and her abilities differently, her old goal no longer satisfies.

Systemic Qualities. The goal-transformation that Julie experienced demonstrates the systemic interaction of the community colleges and their students. The presence and participation of nontraditional students helps to change the way the college conducts its business -- since they are part-time, the administration has to offer more evening, weekend and distance-learning courses to meet their needs. Their presence and participation also affects their own view of themselves as students. Originally convinced she was not "college material," Julie now holds a teaching assistantship at a major graduate school while planning an academic future.

Systemically, nothing happens without causing a counter-action. The shift to a population composed of a larger number of non-traditional students caused many unanticipated changes. The two factors that govern the non-traditional student, part-time attendance and the lower academic self-concept, have had a profound effect on how the community college views itself, an effect that has not been fully recognized.

The growth of part-time students, for example, has resulted in fewer sophomores. The days when a student would enter the college planning to graduate at the end of two years are gone. The increase in part-timers has meant that the average graduating student takes five years to finish. It also means that far fewer remain at the college of entry until graduation. Nationally, fewer than twenty percent of community college students finish two years of attendance. There are, of course, many reasons for this phenomenon: Active recruiting of students who are not likely, for one reason or another, to stay two years; the rise of certificate programs; the cooperative programs sponsored by local business and industry which do not lead to credentials; and, of course, the fact that the largest category of new students, returning adults, are likely because of family or career pressures, to either terminate their education or experience long term stop-outs.

The effects of the growth of part-time students and the move to accommodate them have caused another trend that has resulted in fewer people staying for the full two years: the lack of sophomore level classes. At most colleges, many upper level classes disappeared during the rise of certificate- and other non-transfer programs, which caused a squeeze traditional academic programs. Since all programs are limited to a sixty credit maximum (many certificate programs require only thirty, sending students on their way at the end of one year) and since program coordinators want their students to have as many of those credits as possible within their particular programs, many colleges have cut back on traditional sophomore level requirements and offerings. In fact, the American Association for Community and Junior Colleges claims that the terms freshmen and sophomore are obsolete and has stopped using them.

As a result, more of the academically inclined transfer students are finding themselves forced to leave the community college after one year; the courses they need simply are not there anymore. Mark, a first-year student at an East Coast community college, phrased his dilemma this way: "I don't want to leave here yet. Any way you look at it, academically, financially or emotionally, I'm not sure I'm ready. But I don't have any choice. This school's just not offering the sophomore level courses I need." Timothy, another first year student, agrees. "I'm a journalism major. This school only has the basic intro to journalism course. That's all. If I want to take any courses having anything to do with my major, I have to go somewhere else. I don't want to do it. It means student loans that I didn't want to take on for another year or two, but if the classes aren't here...."

These students feel betrayed by the direction the college is taking. "When they come to the high schools recruiting," Mark says, "they tell you about the small classes, about how student-centered they are. They don't tell you the courses you need aren't there."

The early transfer hurts students in another way. Long range tracking studies indicate that the more credits a student transfers with, the better that student does at his chosen upper division school.

The system, then, has inadvertently worked to drive away many of the academically inclined students and to harm some of the ones it manages to attract. Surprisingly, many schools do not consider either of these facts as a major problem. In fact, some community colleges see no reason to make a serious effort to recruit the better high school students. "As competitive as things are out there," one dean said, "we can't get those students. The universities are getting them. When we do get them, we can't retain them. They leave quickly. It's not worth our time and money to go after students who aren't going to stay with us long enough for us to get a payoff out of it."

The lower ability student. The result of this lack of attention to the better students has been, of course, an increase in less-prepared students, the ones the literature dubs students of lower ability. As stated earlier, the two-year colleges have historically been seen as the natural home for the less equipped; The junior college evolved, in part, as an attempt to get these students to leave the university.

The number of academically ill-equipped students has always been problematic for higher education. As Cross (1971) writes, the history of higher education has been dominated by three views of who should attend college. The *aristocratic* view declares that higher education should be the privilege of rich white males. The *meritocratic* view, on the other hand, states that ability should be the determining factor; those who are able to succeed at college should attend. The third view is the *egalitarian*, which states that the colleges should, as the comprehensive community college did, simply throw open their doors, admitting whoever knocks at the gate, regardless of their background, family income and status, credentials or ability.

Unable to compete for the aristocratic or meritocratic because of its mission, the community college adopted the egalitarian view, opening its doors to students of lesser ability. As a result, Cross says, "the majority of students entering open-door community colleges come from the lower half of high school classes, academically and socioeconomically." (p. 7)

Currently, close to fifty percent of the students entering the community college require remediation, either in reading, composition or math. (The corresponding number in four year schools is thirty percent.) The fact that half of the entering students must be brought up to speed to be able to do the required work indicates that the average community college entrant is not academically prepared to pursue a program. In fact, a large number of entering students who are placed in remedial programs never emerge from them. These students simply do not progress to a point where they can succeed at regular coursework. One suburban school did a long-range tracking study to discover how many of their developmental students successfully completed the remedial English program and went on to pass the first year's English courses. Out of the thousands of students who had entered the program over an eight year period, they discovered, one student had succeeded. Other schools reported similar results. This lack of success would indeed seem to be an indicator of lower ability.

It does not indicate, however, that simply because a student enters from the lower half of her high school class, either academically or socioeconomically, that she is lacking in ability. Julie's experience disproves that assumption. There can be and very often is a distinct difference between lack of preparation and lack of ability. The cases of Robin and Julie serve as evidence for the notion that unprepared students can be able indeed.

Christie's story also illustrates this point. Christie's high school record does not indicate a possibility of success in college; the word she uses to describe her transcript is "dismal." "I didn't do a thing in high school," she said. "I wasn't challenged, but I can't use that for an excuse because I wouldn't have responded to a challenge anyway. I didn't care enough. All I wanted to do was meet up with my friends, cut classes and hang out. I had about as much motivation as a brick."

She came to a community college because her parents wanted her to go to college and "getting in anywhere else wasn't an option." Her first year at the two-year college was simply a repetition of her high school years. She had to take remedial English, math and reading. "I was taking five classes, but three of them were non-credit, so I couldn't see any payoff. I didn't want to be here, didn't see any reason for it. I was just here because my friends were. It was like high school all over again, bagging classes and hanging with my friends."

As was the case with Julie, Christie's academic treadmill was broken by a sudden awakening of interest. "It didn't change till I took a photography course. Then I saw some possibilities. I found I had something in me I wanted to express and a way to express it. At first, I wasn't seeing it as a way to make a living, but it was definitely a way for me to express myself. It was art and I got off on it. I fell in love with the possibilities of light and shadow and I was determined to get good with this camera. At first I just concentrated on photography courses, but then I discovered that the more I knew about me, the more I knew about photography, so that led me into the Humanities. Now I want to know all I can about everything."

Christie graduated with an associate's degree in Applied Art and, after taking a year off to raise money, transferred to an art institute. On any scale, Christie's ability when she entered the school would be measured as low. No one, not even herself, saw her as a candidate for success. When she left, however, the measure was quite different.

Dropping out and stopping out. For all of the successes, however, we must still ask why so many students drop out. Studies suggest that students who stay as those who attend full-time and have higher grade point averages. They are younger, attend during the day and are active in campus activities, ie., traditional students. Non-traditional students are more likely to drop out. There are many reasons why this is the case. For one thing, their goals quite often do not include graduation; therefore they achieve their goals and leave. Since they were there for reasons that required limited time and attendance, they did not stay once their objective was met; staying was never their intention.

For the non-traditional student, any life change can lead to dropping out. A new job, a different shift, a marriage or divorce, a new child - any or all of these can bring a major interruption to a college schedule. Health problems are often cited, as well as changes in a personal financial picture, or in obtaining child care. For people with many demands on their time, a class scheduled at an inconvenient time can be a reason for leaving.

Ironically, the very things that make the community college attractive to non-traditional students also encourage them to drop out. Generally, it is possible to drop a class without penalty up until the end of the semester. It is also possible to attempt a class any number of times. The decision to attend or leave can be made and acted upon in moments. The very flexibility that characterizes the comprehensive community college makes it an easy institution to leave.

Most of the reasons students leave, then, have little or nothing to do with ability. Still, ability dominates the discussions. When we discuss the abilities of students, then, we must keep in mind that demonstrated ability does not always equate with the potential ability. One of the things a community college can do best is to awaken the dormant ability of students.

The awakening of dormant ability might explain the successful transfer rates that community college students have always demonstrated. As far back as 1928, when A. A. Gray wrote the first master's thesis on the community college and declared the institution's students able to transfer successfully, studies have shown that transfer students do at least as well as students who originally entered four year schools.

Studying the rate and success of junior to senior college transfer is tricky, however, because the phenomenon very often does not follow a simple and traditional "two plus two" pattern. A 1994 study by Palmer, Ludwig and Stapleton demonstrates the complexity of the transfer issue. The authors examined data provided by upper division colleges in thirteen states and discovered that transfers were successful but did not fall into the traditional pattern. Only thirty-seven percent of transferring students earned an associate's degree before moving on, for example; most students left after accumulating an average of forty-nine semester hours. Whether they graduated or not, however, most students were able to retain most of their credits upon entering their new institutions. In fact, the data suggests that most transferring students are not impressed by the associate's degree offered by their community college. A full thirty-seven percent accumulated more than sixty hours but either did not complete degree requirements or did not bother to apply for their diplomas. These students could not be categorized as being of lower ability. "The findings also suggest that students who transfer to doctorate-granting institutions are less likely to have earned the associate's degree than those who transfer to non-doctorate institutions." (p. 9) The percentages are worth noting. Fewer than twenty-eight percent of those moving into a doctorate-granting school took an associates degree with them, while forty-three percent of those who went into non-doctorate schools took them.

Lower ability and dormant ability. Plainly, if these students were ever classified as lower-ability, they changed during their study. Dormant abilities became actualized. The two-year college, however, very often mistakes dormant ability for lower ability and, other than provide a place where students can gather until their abilities and interests crystalize, does nothing to increase the level of ability. By trying to be all things to all people, it aims, like television, for the lowest common denominator and, also like television, becomes cynical. It assumes the worst about its students and, in assuming the worst, tends to bring out the worst in them.

As one registrar put it, "the administration here just wants warm bodies in the seats, that's all. If we registered a herd of cattle and they didn't do well in classes, the dean would be sending us memos demanding that we find ways to retain the cows. Get another semester out of them, that's what they want."

Academics who discuss the community college are correct when they speak of non-traditional students and students of lesser ability. However, they draw the wrong conclusions. Because they look at the students and the school from a linear perspective, they have a static view of both, assuming that schools and their students are always what they are at their points of origin. The systemic interaction between two-year colleges and their students, however, is complex, multifaceted, and misunderstood. The interaction deals with potential.

Many of the community college's constituents bring old baggage to the college with them - a history of failure, for example, or the negative self-concept that failure can create. Given an opportunity to discover that the past does not rule the present, they learn from systemic interaction with the student-centered school that who they were is not who they are. The potential that previous schooling buried can surface and a student can actualize that potential and become "college material." This transformation happens frequently and is, in fact, one of the best facets of the community college.

The school, therefore, is a different place for each student and is actually a different place at different times for every student. Students, then, are in the act of becoming. To judge Robin, Julie and Christie by the attitudes and personalities demonstrated at the time they entered the school is to simply see the static qualities and to refuse to see the growth that is just below the surface. The school changed these students and these students in turn changed the school.

Until the colleges understand the systemic interaction they share with their students, neither the schools nor their students will live up to their potential.

Chapter Seven:

Governing the Community College

Let us begin with a statement from Bensimon, Neumann and Birnbaum:

> The following three statements are probably universally accepted as truths: There is a general consensus that higher education has a leadership crisis. Strong, effective leadership is necessary for a strong, effective institution. Most academic leaders are unschooled and unsure about what constitutes effective leadership. (p. xv)

George Keller states the case in an even stronger voice:

> There is now a stalemate in the exercise of power on the American campus. University management is now in shackles. While the balance of power in our Madisonian federal government has been tilting since the thirties toward the executive branch, presidential power in U. S. higher education has gradually diminished before the buildup of strong faculty power and, since the sixties, the rising power of students and outside agencies. (p. 27)

Cohen and March are less diplomatic in their discussion, saying, "The American college or university is a prototypic organized anarchy. It does not know what it is doing." (1974, p. 3)

Since community colleges adopted the university form of management back in generation two, what is true for the universities is also true for the community colleges. It is safe to say, therefore, that the majority of the nation's community colleges are as poorly managed as universities. Scholars of the community college have long decried the poor level of governance, just as those of the universities have discussed the poor administration there. On both levels, the diminishment of administrative effectiveness has become a familiar and oft-told story. As far back as 1963, Clark Kerr used the metaphor of competing nations to describe the various parties to governance on college campuses, declaring that several "nations" exist at every college, consisting of students, faculty, alumni, trustees, and public groups. Each, claims Kerr, has its territory, its jurisdiction, its own way of operating. These groups compete, rather than cooperate, since each is more concerned with its own welfare than the overall welfare of the schools. Kerr is not the only person to describe this state of tension existing in colleges. Most writers on administration agree with him, veering from the position his statement describes primarily to declare that the situation has gotten worse since he wrote his critique. Governance of colleges, both four- and two-year, is generally viewed as ineffective, wasteful, and self-defeating. In fact, in discussions, the operative term describing college administration is "crisis." (Keller, 1983, Bennett, 1984)

The myths and fallacies of college governance. How did the administration of colleges get into this state? George Keller declares that the roots of the poor management lie in the myths surrounding the operation of colleges, myths that faculty, students and as often as not, since they are former faculty members, most of the administrators themselves accept as truth. The major myth is that "each college or university is close to an Athenian democracy of professional scholars who know each other and share a bundle of values and aspirations which they practice in their institutional lives." (p. 30) These professional scholars, the myth goes, are self-governing. Collectively, they make the decisions that enable them to operate. They also police themselves. The college, then, is a free society, a commune that demonstrates the major quality that most communes over the ages have traditionally lacked: the ability to sustain operations.

A minimal amount of governance might be necessary, communards agree. Someone has to keep track of students, make sure the books are ordered, schedule classes and protect academic freedom. Those who are entrusted with the power to do these acts have to be carefully watched, however, to prevent them from overstepping their bounds.

The people who do even minimal governing are viewed skeptically because the faculty is not convinced that they are either needed not trustworthy. Most administrators are former teachers and that might be part of the problem. Once people move out of the classroom, many faculty members feel, they develop different loyalties, a new agenda that runs counter to their old teaching values. Keller states that three historical beliefs are responsible for this suspicion. First, there is the belief in the Golden Age. This belief centers on the myth that there once was a time:

> when a condition of faculty control and Athenian democracy did exist on most campuses. Before the rise of bureaucracy, business, accounting, and efficiency experts, and power-hankering presidents, there was a happier, collegial age - to which campuses should return. (p. 31)

The second belief is that a model does exist. In England, the stately universities
have always enjoyed full self-government, the myth says; they were communities of scholars who tolerated no encroachment on their turf, not even from people within their community. Government operated by consensus and all decisions were the result of open discussion. Since that model exists, American schools should emulate it. The myth is strengthened by the additional belief that this ideal situation also existed in the German universities. Since these schools provided the models for America's first institutions of higher education, we should also adopt their manner of complete self-government.

Keller points out that all of these beliefs are fallacious. During what we think of as the "Golden Age," presidents were in fact quite strong, ruling almost by fiat. A 1908 report by the Carnegie Foundation for the Advancement of Teaching claimed that "the powers of the American college president resembled those of the president of a railroad." (Keller, p. 31) The beliefs in the British and German models are equally rooted in fantasy. The British universities were noted for apathy, weakness and complacency, coupled with a smugness and sense of righteousness that led the major schools, Cambridge and Oxford, to ignore every major advance in knowledge of the time, such as the rise of science and technology. They were not self-governing as they were self-insulating. The result was a group of schools desperately out of touch with its own time, a collection of institutions devoted to passing down a vision of a past that never was. The German universities were no more autonomous. They were, in fact, closely controlled and managed by the state; professors were civil servants under the rule of a state-appointed "Curator." They achieved academic freedom only by avoiding controversy. Perhaps they did not attempt to exclude reality, as the British did, but they definitely only admitted those aspects of it which were safe.

In their beliefs concerning self-government, therefore, American colleges were as blind to truth as the British schools. Regardless of the falsity of their sustaining beliefs, they allowed those beliefs to govern relations between faculty and administrators. To a large extent, the beliefs still have a profound influence, but that fact does not fully explain why a state of tension exists among the involved parties on college campuses.

Poor governance. To understand why these tensions exist, we must consider also that most community colleges are abominably governed. They always have been. In his 1931 study, Eells took note of the two central facts: each community college was jury-rigging its own management system and most of the colleges were poorly managed. He attributed the poor governance of community colleges to the lack of standardization in the institution's governing structures, reporting that even in the early stages of its history, the two-year college's forms of administration were

> Too varied and comprehensive to be treated completely in a work such as this. Many of the methods of organization and administration of junior colleges are common to four-year colleges and universities on the one hand or to high schools on the other. (354)

College governance was not effective when Eels wrote in 1931 and it is not now. The diversity of forms he pointed to might be one reason for the poor performance, but they are not the only, or even the most important, one. Other studies offer different perspectives on the problem. For example, in 1987, when the Carnegie Foundation for the Advancement of Teaching conducted a study of colleges in America, they expressed dissatisfaction with the way they were administrated:

> In reality, the decision-making processes on most campuses are not working very well. Although faculty members feel a deep sense of loyalty to their professions, they are less committed to the institutions where they work. We also found that, almost without exception, the role of students in campus decision-making is not taken seriously in higher education. (Boyar, p. 325)

The Commission wrote that in earlier days, back during the last century, college governance was a simple matter. The president ruled, running the school as though he owned it. His voice was the institution's voice and he was deferred to by the faculty and the student body. It was a calmer time and social roles were more rigid than they are now. A system in which a benevolent dictator took charge could be effective in those simpler times. It was simple for one man to speak for a college because the nation's schools and faculties were smaller - in 1859, one of the largest schools in the nation, the University of Michigan, had twenty faculty members. A unified voice was not difficult to achieve and neither was a common goal difficult to visualize. As Boyar points out, however, "as universities became larger and more complex, confusion about decision-making increased and relations between faculty and administration became more obscure." (p. 236)

The new complexity created confusion and division between faculty and administrators, an inevitable result when it is considered that faculty members learned not to fully trust administrators; interests diverged as the complexity of operations increased. The administrative crisis was created. The we-versus-they situation that had always lurked just beneath the surface came to the forefront as faculty grew remote from and more distrustful of their administrations; as the Bennett report did earlier, the Carnegie Foundation report speaks of adversarial relationships between the two parties, along with the almost total exclusion of students from the governing process.

The situation on community college campuses today is one of skepticism. Sixties-bred faculties tend to lack good-will toward their presidents and deans. They often to describe their administrators as managers or bureaucrats and claim that the deans and presidents do not have insight into the roles and natures of the schools they administer. They feel the two groups have different goals. One teacher reported, "For a bunch of people who used to be teachers, they don't have the first idea what teaching is about. Did they forget or did they never know?"

Models of governance. One problem with the management of community colleges is that, as is the case with nearly everything else about the institution, it takes so many different forms. The pattern is that there is no true pattern. Models abound. Merton (1963) describes a bureaucratic model based on rational principles and characterized by a hierarchical structure, with top-down communication and authority, in which the president or her representatives issues statements which the masses on the lower ends of the hierarchy obey. One person calls the tune and everyone dances. A major goal of all parties in a bureaucratic model is the avoidance of conflict. Millett (1962) offers a collegial model, which tries to keep alive the myth of self-government associated with the British universities. Under this structure a community of near equals share decisions-making power; all parties (or their duly elected representatives) meet to determine policy, procedures and rules. The collegial model values harmony and unity. Consensus and participation are the dominant features of the model and authority does not rest in one person's hands. The tune is discussed until all agree on what is to be played. Then each party does her own variation of the dance.

The goal of both the bureaucratic and collegial models is, of course, the building of cooperation among the various parties. In the event that this goal becomes impossible to achieve and conflict between parties achieves dominance, Baldridge (1971) suggests that a political model comes into existence. This model operates the same way politics operate in the larger society and features different interest groups which advocate for their own vision, competing with each other to influence the final decision. The model is neither hierarchal nor collegial; both of those models assume a certain degree of cooperation and the political model lacks that quality. Each party has his own song and fights to get the others to do his dance.

The patchwork nature of governance. Despite the fact that these descriptions suggest that the models are complete and readily functional, the fact is that none of them exists in a pure form on community college campuses. In truth, the governance of colleges is a patchwork quilt that is never finished. It is made up of unequal and changing patches of each model. Actual governance, as opposed to theoretical, is difficult to describe because it does not know what it is.

What can be said about the governance of the colleges is that they generally follow hierarchical models and are ruled in a top-town manner, with information flowing - usually on paper - from a group of managers to the other groups on campus: faculty, classified staff, and students. Decisions are made either by fiat or by compromise. The guiding principle for administration is generally pragmatism; community colleges are not ruled by either theory or principles deriving from values.

Why is community college governance such a patchwork? One major reason might be tradition; it is patchwork because it has always been patchwork. The tradition was inadvertently established early in this century and the colleges have been faithfully following it ever since. E. Q. Brothers (1928) did an early study of administrative models, taking a look at eighty-six different institutions. He found that the administrative methods differed considerably. In 27 of the schools, the dean reported to a high school principal, suggesting that in the eyes of the community, the college was of lesser value than the high school. Indeed, in twenty-two other schools, the dean *was* the high school principal. He simply did double duty, running a community college in his spare time. In twenty-five schools, the dean reported directly to the superintendent of schools, while in four, the superintendent doubled as the dean. Two schools allowed the assistant principal of the local high school to simultaneously serve as dean of the community college. In all of the eighty-three reporting schools, not one had established a board of trustees. None saw the community college as an independent entity. In fact, only twenty-five of the deans felt that the schools should be independent.

Even though the majority of schools were happy with the ways in which they were administered, Brothers concluded that they should not be. In order to achieve their potential, the colleges should be independent, he reported, if only because the students resented the paternalistic practices of high school administrators, who did not understand colleges. Since community colleges and high schools had different aims and different practices, he felt, they should be administered as separate entities.

Most states eventually adopted Brothers' recommendations, but the separation of powers did not end the administrative mess; the tradition continues. Although most schools today operate separately from high schools, there is still no uniform pattern. In twenty states, the state board of education is in direct authority while another fifteen utilize separate state boards created especially to administer community colleges. In seven states, the same board governs universities and community colleges while others use more localized control. Regardless of which agency has ultimate authority, most schools operate under the supervision of a board of trustees. (Blocker, Plummer & Richardson, 1965)

Under this system, the board outlines policy and makes major funding and budgeting decisions. The day to day operation of the schools is the responsibility of a president hired by the board and who answers directly to the members. According to Keller, the president should spend at least fifty percent of his time administering the campus, although "some unwisely spend nine-tenths of their time on it." (p. 122) The president, Keller feels, is responsible for operating a "good" institution and schools are considered good if things run smoothly; buildings and grounds are attractive, students are recruited successfully, faculty are energetic, approachable and productive, the library works as it should, courses run smoothly and alumni are active. Well-administered places, he writes, "are efficient campuses, where limited funds are spent with maximum effect and with a taste and manner befitting...." (p. 123) These items are basic, Keller emphasizes. The president, however, should not simply keep the plant running; she should also be a manager of change.

Beneath the president is a line of administrators, the various deans and supervisors, who oversee specific aspects of the campus operation. They carry out the presidential directives in order to make certain the campus meets the criteria for good. Beneath the various deans are the division and department heads who oversee the faculty. On paper the chain of command is usually as rigid as the military's. In practice, however, it is frequently ignored, sidetracked or undermined. Because in many cases each party perceives itself as having an interest that it must protect from the others, a political model often emerges, extenuating the conflict between faculty, who tend to feel that little or no administration is needed, and administrators, who naturally tend to disagree.

Faculty-administrative schisms. Because the governance of community colleges is as complex and confused as that of universities, the same faculty-administration schism exists. One faculty member at a suburban Massachusetts community college describes the schism at his school in these words:

> In the community college ... there is less and less faculty involvement in the total daily operation of the college. When I first came here, there were about the same number of full-time faculty as we have now, maybe five more. We had two counselors for the whole school, two librarians, maybe four deans, one president, eight secretaries and that was it. The faculty did everything. We counseled the students, we did this, we did that, and we were just involved in the whole of things....
> Now there is a structure. We have nine full-time counselors. Every dean has an assistant dean. Some of the deans have two assistant deans and an associate dean. All the directors have an assistant director - director of financial aid, associate director of financial aid, director of student affairs.... So what started to be a college of one hundred and five teachers, and eighteen staff, and a president and four deans is now a president and fifteen deans over one hundred staff members of the college. So the staff has actually reached the point where, exclusive of the secretaries, the staff for the college is actually as large as the teaching faculty, and it [the college] has compartmentalized and pigeonholed job descriptions a lot more and has made it harder to function as a team. (Seidman, pp. 42-43)

Top administrators have also recognized the distrust and skepticism that many faculty feel toward the governing bodies. One newly installed president, aware that managers and other interested parties on campus were often at odds because of differing views of the history, culture and values of the schools they were supposed to govern, was careful in his inaugural remarks to say that he thought "... many administrators in transition are too eager to supervise change without fully listening to the history of the institution and the individuals whose collective they seek to lead to realization. (quoted in Roueche, Baker lll & Rose, p 113)

The result of this administrative history distrust, competition and formlessness is the formation of a genuine crisis. The university's administrative crisis is easy to understand. It originated in its history. It grew out of the college's views of its traditions and its links to the past. Tradition and history do not explain the community college crisis, however. The community college has no deep-seated, centuries old past. It sprang into being as a brand new form at the turn of the twentieth century and has never shared the university's traditions.

Origins of the administrative crisis. Where, then, did the community college's administrative crisis come from? It can be traced to the institution's failure to recognize its systemic qualities while it was growing. During generation one, the public junior colleges did not present much of an administrative challenge. Viewed as extensions of the local high schools and frequently housed in high school buildings, it was natural for the units to be managed by people trained in the administration of secondary schools. The relevant city or county board of education operated the schools, assigning a principal to oversee the day to day workings. Since the high schools provided a reasonably efficient and cost effective model, there was no reason to look elsewhere for administrative patterns. This form of management served adequately because the schools were not really, at this point, complex operations.

The growth of professionalism during generation two, however, caused a shifting of administrative models as the two-year college, like a self-made man ashamed of his poverty-stricken origins, shook off its affiliation with the high schools. The new professional organizations were formed specifically to end for all time any association with the high schools and to gain professionalism by positioning the two-year schools directly beside the four-year colleges. These organizations largely succeeded and, as they gained political clout, the political domains that were responsible for the schools - state, county or local governments - formed commissions of higher education to govern the schools.

Local school boards affiliated with the high school administrations disappeared, to be replaced by the sprawling myriad of forms described earlier. The changes did not lead to clarity or uniformity. Blocker, Plummer and Richardson reported that only twenty states still had community colleges under the direct supervision of a state board of education. In six others, a state superintendent of education headed them up. By 1992, when Tollefson and Fountain studied the situation, only seven states still let a state board of education directly govern their community colleges. Schools in sixteen states utilized state boards of higher education, while those in seventeen states were operated by college boards and schools in another seven fell under their state's university systems. The others have variations on the board of trustees system.

As stated, the various types of boards most often operate by macromanaging, determining broad policies and hiring presidents do the micromanage. The presidents carry out the board's broad directives, handling the day to day operation of the campuses. They strive to create Keller's good campuses. As noted in chapter three, whatever form these boards take, they are generally close and responsive to the local communities they represent. Therefore they have a local, rather than global, vision.

Although some states have always had boards of trustees, most adopted this form of governance during generation three's transformation from junior college to the community college. Success, then, changed both the mission and the administrative makeup of the schools. This record of success caused national politicians to take notice. When the Truman administration resolved to extend opportunity for higher education in America, the positive track record of the two-year schools caused the commission appointed by the president to recognize that these schools were best equipped to carry out its stated goal of wider educational access for the whole community.

It was under the prodding of the Truman administration that the junior college widened its scope of operations, becoming the community college. With this shift in its mission came a corresponding shift in governing power. A new and expanded scope of operations required a different way of looking at the schools, their missions and their operations. Boards of trustees, whose members were often not educators, were incapable of taking the schools down the Truman tracks. Where before the boards had held the power, driving the train while their appointed presidents shoveled coal, now the boards could no longer occupy the engineer's seat. The Truman Commission's mandate was a map that only the presidents, who, unlike the board members, were educators, could read. With its acceptance, the presidents, knowing the way to the destination, donned the engineer's cap.

Evidently, there sense of direction was not as strong as the presidents believed it to be. Events proved them to be not certain of the route either. They led to the community college's administrative crisis.

Leadership and management. To accomplish a complete shift in mission, purpose and identity requires a person who can articulate the vision and inspire people to bring it into being. In generation three, it became more important to have a vision and the wisdom to make others share it, believe in it and crave its manifestation than to demonstrate the bureaucratic skills necessary to do routine management.

Consider the difference between a mom and pop store and Wal-Mart. To create and operate a chain of superstores demanded infinitely more than running a single Main Street store. The community college was being transformed into Wal-Mart. To pull off the alteration required new ways of perceiving the field. Before Truman, administrators simply managed; they carried out the limited and mundane directives of the board. After Truman, managing was no longer enough. The new role required a new vision and providing vision is a task beyond the scope of a manager; it requires a leader.

Therefore, we might think of generation three as the period of the leader, a period when different qualities were sought and rewarded. As Bennis and Nanus (1985) write:

> There is a profound difference between management and leadership, and both are important. "To manage" means "to bring about, to accomplish, to have charge of or responsibility for, to conduct." "Leading" is "influencing, guiding in direction, course, action, opinion." The distinction is crucial. *Managers are people who do things right and leaders are people who do the right thing.* (p. 21. Quotes and italics in the original)

The major difference between leaders and managers, Bennis and Nanus declare, is in the way they see their roles. Leaders have a wider focus. They don't watch the engine as much as they do the direction of the tracks. They concern themselves with why their organization is making the journey in the first place and always question the direction in which they are travelling in. Bennis and Nanus call these people vision-oriented. Leaders create "new ideas, new policies, new methodologies." (p. 23) as much as they keep an eye out for the eventual destination.

One man, hired as the president of a Florida Junior College in the late fifties, said, "The school was running just fine when I came in, but the board made clear that running it wasn't enough. My job was to change the entire paradigm. In a very real sense, my job was to create a new school out of the old one." To make such radical changes in an operation requires more than management.

Tucker (1984) defined leadership as "... the ability to influence or motivate a group of people to work willingly toward a given goal under a specific set of circumstances." (p. 41) This ability is exactly what is required to change a paradigm and, as the words of the Florida president show, the task in generation three was to change paradigms.

Transactional and transformational leadership. To change paradigms, in fact, does not simply require leadership skills; it requires skills of a very specific type. We will discuss leadership in depth in the final chapter. For the moment, we will be content to highlight the topic by exploring the distinctions between two types of leadership, transactional and transformational. To understand the significance, it is worthwhile to remember that while management might be unilateral, all leadership is bilateral; to lead means to interact with and influence others. The difference between transactional and transformational leadership is the difference between the quality of the interaction between parties.

According to Burns (1978) transactional leadership is characterized by a relationship between people based on an exchange, which may be political, social, economic or psychological. This style of leadership centers on a bargain, stated or implied. All of the involved parties negotiate a payoff; they then work together to accomplish a desired goal in order to receive the negotiated benefit. Transactional leadership, therefore, usually builds partnerships and coalitions. These groups, however, last only until the desired goal is reached; these are only temporary partnerships as the transaction is a temporary state. After the goal is reached, if the work is to continue, a new bargain must be struck.

Transformational leadership, on the other hand, unites people by increasing levels of motivation and morality. The goal becomes not a benefit to pocket or a goal to be achieved but something that all parties own. Transformational leadership does not deal in, say, monthly sales quotas and contests, with negotiated rewards for achievement. As Bensimon, Neumann and Birnbaum (1989) state, "leaders and followers become fused under transformational leadership, rather than separate but related as under transactional leadership." (p. 10).

According to Bennis and Nanus (1985) the transformational leader exhibits four qualities:

1: attention through vision, which means having a clear agenda and keeping the desired result in mind. The leader keeps his own attention focused on the goal and also creates an atmosphere where everyone else is similarly focused. The goal becomes everyone's rather than simply his; no one gets sidetracked or drifts off onto another track because of uncertainty or disagreement.

2: Achieving through communication. The transformational leader does not rely on memos and policy statements. She values true and deep communication and utilizes metaphors, images and models. She does not rely only on top down communication, but encourages its flow in all directions and recognizes that good ideas can originate in unlikely places.

3: Gaining trust through positioning. The transformational leader models the attitudes and behaviors she expects out of others. She recognizes that leaders get back what they put out; if she desires a focused campus, she must not only be focused, but must demonstrate that focus in both public and private encounters with other team-members.

4: The deployment of self through positive self-regard. The transformational leader spends most of her time dealing with people and deals with them in terms of mutual respect and trust. Not only is she not cloistered in her office, she is out among her people, demonstrating that both she and they are worthy of respect. As one president said, "Drop by a man's office and chat with him. You'll be amazed what a difference it makes."

As generation three took shape, management could no longer handle the responsibilities that now belonged to the schools. The task had changed; it was now to transform the school from a junior college to a community college. To do so required a new vision. That was why the president of the Florida community college quoted earlier was hired; his job was to see things differently. To do so also required the use of transformational leadership, which

> is unique and has more distinguishable behaviors associated with its conceptualization. It builds on the human need for meaning, it creates institutional purpose, it involves vision and judgment, it involves values and the shaping of values in others, and it requires of the leader and the follower the ability to transcend their own limited views and perform beyond what is normally expected. Transformational leaders seek to arouse and satisfy higher needs in the follower, to engage the full person of the follower. (Baker lll, Rouesche, and Gillett-Karam, 1990, p. 38)

Because of the quality of the leadership, generation three is remembered by staffers who were a part of it as the glory years. One veteran faculty members remembered those days this way:

> Those days were the last time I trusted the administration. Back then, we all felt we were in this thing together. It was crusade and we were all united on the side of good. We were close, tight. Everybody was a part of every decision. Today, everything's done by memos. Every day I get a stack of

memos telling me how things are going to be. I don't even know all the people who send them.

A former dean of students agrees:

There was a sense that we were all together doing great and important work. All of us, whether we were students, faculty, administrators, or support staff, knew each other, liked each other, and respected each other. We made every major decision together. We thought in terms of people, not FTE's [full-time equivalents] And you can't say it was because we were small. The college grew from seven thousand to twelve thousand during that period. By the time I retired in 1986, it was all different. I didn't feel I belonged there any more.

The system as a factor in governance. As the former dean's words indicate, most generation three schools were run in a manner that was sensitive to their systemic nature. All units of the system were involved in all major decisions and each member felt that his part was vital and recognized. By the time generation four was established the situation changed. The move to comprehensiveness had been solidified. As a result, the face of the community college had been fundamentally altered and the institution had won its seat at the higher education table. In fact, it had won a quiet revolution, emerging as the dominant force: by generation four more than fifty percent of undergraduate students attended two-year schools.

The effects of a failure of vision. Any transformation, though, is systemic and reverberates throughout the entire system. The vision of the shapers of the comprehensive community college turned out to be incomplete; they did not anticipate all of the effects of their work. They failed to see an obvious point: transforming the colleges would also transform the student population. In retrospect, the change was predictable; since the purpose of the schools was altered, it stands to reason that the student body would be altered also. It was during this period, for example, that the number of full-time transfer students began to decline and the number of part-time adult nontransfer students increased.

Many reasons have been advanced for the drying up of the full-time lake. Most of them are at least partially accurate. For one, the economy was changing; more people could afford four year schools and chose to attend them. For another, there were simply fewer traditional students available and four-year schools began competing actively for students they would have rejected in the past; many of these students had been the natural constituency of the community college. A third reason was that the systemic change from junior college to the newer comprehensive community college led many schools to neglect the full-time traditional student, rationalizing that those students did not belong at the two-year college in the first place. Many administrators, reflecting the thinking of the major professional associations, began simply paying lip service to academic programs and the students they attracted while actively working to build up the technical and vocational programs that they viewed as a more immediate source of bodies in the chairs.

Some of these administrators felt non-transfer students were the more natural constituency of the two-year colleges. Many contemporary thinkers continue to advocate this view and advocate that the community college recognize their own particular view of educational reality by shifting emphasis away from the transfer function:

> A college prep-baccalaureate-degree program is certainly the road to excellence for many individuals, and our schools and community colleges must help these students prepare for this direction in life better than ever before. Indeed, community colleges are actively pursuing programs to encourage and motivate more community college students to press on to the baccalaureate degree. But we must constantly remind ourselves that the majority of our students will never earn a baccalaureate degree. What about the ordinary student? What can we offer him or her? (Parnell, 1985, p. 7)

Parnell's solution for the "ordinary student" is, as previously stated, a tech-prep program that bypasses the academic transfer program altogether. His book describing his program, *The Neglected Majority*, was issued by the American Association of Community Colleges, an organization of which he served as president and which has a long history of advocating terminal occupational programs at the expense of transfer programs. As far back as 1965, Brick reported that the Association had made a deliberate decision to move in that direction. He quoted C.C. Colvert, an earlier president of the association, as saying,

> Had not we of the junior college been so busy trying to offer courses which would get our graduates into the senior colleges instead of working and offering appropriate and practical courses - terminal courses - for the vast majority of junior college students, we have thought to ask for, and as a result of having asked, received the privilege of training these young people. (p. 121)

In a more recent book, *The Diverted Dream*, co-authored with Karabel, Brick charged that the AAJC had a long and sustained history of deliberately working to move the community college to a position more in line with its own vision of terminal education. By generation four, all of the forces were in line to help the AAJC's dream become reality. The move toward a greater comprehensiveness and the shortage of traditional students created a new emphasis on terminal programs.

From leadership to management. The new emphasis, of course, leads to a fourth reason for the decline in full-time traditional academic students; the community college no longer had very much to offer them.

By generation four, not just the schools' programs and students were different; their governance had changed also. Faced with competition from four year schools for the best students and faced with a changing mission, the community college needed a different kind of administrator - a person who was capable of *maintaining*, a person who could hold onto the gains that had been previously made. Vision no longer got the job done. During this time, vision was not perceived as being as important as bureaucratic skills. Leaders were replaced by managers, people who did things right rather than doing the right thing.

The replacement of leaders, who united people around a common vision, with managers, who placed whole structures of complex policies between themselves and the other parties and enforced those policies, brought on the adversarial position that Carnegie Foundation discovered. It also added to the administrative complexity. If an administrative form that is perceived as hostile is saddled with complexity, the result will be an administration that becomes "an ineffective Rube Goldberg-like arrangement." (Boyar, 1987, p. 242) Removing leadership by reverting to management had an inevitable result; it eroded trust, which, of course, eroded the shared vision.

Diminishing the level and quality of vision was inevitable. Protecting a finished portrait, however, does not require the same sort of perception as the painting of that portrait called for. To hold on to previously made gains requires a different set of skills. "When I was hired," said the current president of the Florida community college that had wanted radical change, "I was told by the board that my job was to keep it running smoothly and to carry out their directives. The president before me had made a lot of initiatives and they didn't want that anymore."

Maintenance does not create a sense of visionary excitement, nor does it lead to a renewed sense of mission which causes growth, purpose and meaning. The shift from leadership to management came at an unfortunate time and had, as we shall see, serious implications which must be recognized and addressed before a fifth generation of history attempts to take the community college into the twenty-first century.

To recognize the the limitations of the ability of management to plan and execute a movement into the twenty-first century, we need only consider some of the issues that will dominate the community college in the early years of that century. Deggan (1989) lists them:

1: Increasing competition within higher education. Not only is competition among colleges and universities tightening, an increased thrust for students is coming from other quarters. The armed forces, training centers within business and industry, and other types of schools or organizations, such as Sylvan Learning Centers, are invading territory that used to belong to the community college. The developmental function, which touches such a large percentage of current students, is especially vulnerable.

2: Funding and managing technological developments. Computerization and the other new methods of transmitting information have created a need to re-think of "nearly every aspect of higher education." (p. 203) To achieve excellence in learning will require technological equipment, skilled personnel and new linkages and consortia. It will also require a careful consideration of the human qualities of education. To leap into the use of technology simply because it is available and faddish will be an expensive mistake - one that many community colleges are currently making. The approach to and use of technology will present a series of problems and issues that must be faced.

3: Changing student clientele. Not only are there fewer eighteen year olds available, the ethnic makeup of that cohort is rapidly changing. African-Americans, Hispanics and Asians are increasing, while the Caucasian population is shrinking. Ethnicity is not the only change on the horizon. The nontraditional student is increasing even more. All of these differences in student populations will present new challenges. The community college will have to educate student populations that they have not traditionally been skilled at communicating with, much less teaching.

4: Increasing faculty shortages. Everyone who entered the system during the fantastic growth of the sixties is ready to leave it. Faculties consist of veteran, older teachers; the tight times of the eighties and nineties meant that replacement was most often accomplished by the use of adjuncts. "A large percentage of faculty will have to be replaced within the next ten years, and colleges need to plan for that now through more attention to staffing patterns, staff development, and new roles and the use of technology." (p. 204)

5: Growing state control. States are becoming much more reluctant to turn over huge sums of money to schools without overseeing what the institutions do with it. Keller reports that over seventy percent of schools cannot start a new program without state approval. In many cases, perceived fiscal and operational abuses by the colleges are responsible for this trend. In other cases, it results from the desire of politicians to increase their power. Whatever the point of origin, it will be necessary for college administrators to either fight or accommodate this trend toward less autonomy.

Fourth-generation management cannot deal successfully with these issues and trends. In order to maximally function in the twenty-first century, it will be essential for the schools to develop transformational leadership.

Chapter Eight:

The Community College in the Twenty-first Century

Despite its problems and despite the issues facing it in the near future, there is no question the community college is one of the most important forces in contemporary higher education. Indeed, it is no longer possible to conceive of higher education without considering the two-year college. The institution will undoubtably continue to be a prime force, but if it is to achieve its full potential by building on the success that it has had, changes will have to be made. The sharp focus of purpose has largely been lost; today the institution is like a mismanaged declining retail shop that, since it cannot sell its main product, has taken on different lines of novelty items in an attempt to survive. If it is Wal-Mart, it is Wal-Mart in the directionless days immediately after the founder, Sam Walton, died. The two-year college is drifting aimlessly. The inevitable result of drifting for too long is too run aground. The community college, which is drifting toward an uncertain, impossible to predict future, circling without a clear direction, is too important to the nation's future to allow it to meet that fate.

The need for a new way of thinking. Obviously, if the community college is to be all that it is capable of becoming, its tendency to drift must be corrected. How can that goal be achieved? Before taking any set of corrective actions, a new way of thinking will be necessary. So far, we have been applying linear thinking to the problems. Linear thinking uses traditional problem solving techniques. Faced with a problem, the linear thinker looks to the past and asks what action was taken the last time he was faced with this sort of problem. He then attempts to apply the same type of action that he applied in the past. If it worked once, he believes, it will work again. For the linear thinker, the future is built directly on the past.

The problem, of course, is that the corrective action did not work the first time. If it had, it would not be necessary to try the same action again. Since the present time is not the past and since each situation is unique, new corrective actions will be required.

Systems thinking provides new actions. The systems thinker recognizes that situations, problems, and issues do not directly recur; when they repeat, they are not the same, but are actually transformations of their previous incarnations. Systems thinking recognizes that each situation is new and must therefore be handled in a new way. For the systems thinker, each situation grows out of a specific systemic set of interactions. Since these systemic interactions are never precisely the same, the situation isn't either.

New thinking leads to new actions. A new way of thinking is essential, then because new actions are impossible without new thinking. The first necessary step in developing a new way of thinking is to recognize that the fourth generation of the institution's history, with its emphasis on self-protective, self-maintenance management, is over. Without our being aware of it, the situation in which the community college finds itself has changed. Nearly everything the college is, as well as nearly every issue the institution faces, is different from what the colleges dealt with in the fourth generation.

While assuming that we have been standing still, we've been on a circuitous journey. The destination was, of course, the fifth generation of community college history and, without being fully conscious that we were going anywhere, we have arrived. The problem, of course, is in our lack of awareness. We have drifted into the new period of history without seeing any of the signposts; since we did not know we were going anywhere, we could not know where we were going.

A Renewal of Vision. It is obvious that if we intend to arrive at any chosen destination, we must have good maps; we definitely need to know the direction. Further, we must have people who are both able to blaze the trail and to inspire the rest of us to keep moving when the trek gets difficult. When our vision becomes obscured, we must find or develop people who are capable to helping us regain clarity. During the third generation, these people were present in leadership capacities on our campuses, but when the emphasis shifted to maintenance during the fourth generation, there was no longer any place for them. Since the fourth generation did not reward them, they are not currently in place on the campuses, as they need to be. As a result, the two year college currently stands in desperate need of leadership.

Without strong leadership to correct the drift, the two-year colleges try to journey in too many directions at once. The frantic and unfocused activity is the result of a fundamental error in perception; like television programmers, the schools mistook quantity for quality. Simple popularity became the indicator for success. They counted heads and if the count was up, they considered themselves successful. Since numbers were seen as the indicator of success, should the figures happen to be down, they made moves that would attract more students. This reliance on numbers changed all the definitions. During the fourth generation, a good program became defined as one that attracted people - whether it offered them very much or not. The schools tried to give the public what it wanted instead of what it needed. Like a bad retail store, they pandered instead of leading. At this writing, therefore, the schools are spread much too thin; they are living up to Hutchins' 1954 warning about the dangers of trying to be all things to all people. They have lost their vision.

As a result, we can say one thing with certainty: the community college in the twenty-first century will not be what it is today. To attempt to stay in the same place is to become Ames instead of Wal-Mart; the bankruptcy will be huge and public. New leadership will be necessary to avoid that fate and that leadership will have to be both systemic and transformational.

Only the fresh perspective that transformational leadership will provide can restore a clear and unique vision and restoring the vision is centrally important. If that does not happen, then no other measures will be matter; they will not be effective.

The Importance of Vision. Vision is the key to effective systemic change. According to Bennis and Nanus, (1984) vision creates focus. If it is present in the leadership, if an institution has leaders who are compelled by their own vision, then these leaders

> do not have to coerce people to pay attention; they are so intent on what they are doing that, like a child completely absorbed with creating a sand castle in a sandbox, they draw others in. (p. 28)

Vision *grabs,* the authors say. "Initially, it grabs the leader and management of attention enables others to also get on the bandwagon." (p. 28) Visionary leadership that grabs and creates the enthusiasm in others that makes them want to sign on is essential if the fifth generation is to make genuine alterations in the fabric of the community college.

The vision that will be required for the fifth generation will center on the recognition of the systemic nature of the community college. It will be devoted to helping to strengthen that system.

Linear and Systemic Models. The leadership required by the community college will of necessity be transformational because its task will be to transform the shared perception of the community college into what it has always been. It will help people in the colleges recognize that they are systems. Therefore, it will transform the perceptions of the schools from linear models to a systemic one. The linear model will no longer serve. What renders it ineffective is the fact that it continues the old management mistake of dividing the interested parties into leaders and followers, the empowered and the disempowered. It creates competing factions, instead of a unified group.

Should a model consider the administration to be made up of leaders while considering the faculty, staff and students to be there in order to serve the administration's will by following, then power is drained and the resulting efforts to educate will be harmed. Similarly, should faculty, staff and students not understand the necessary role of administration, the educative function will be similarly harmed.

It must be considered also that not just the faculty, staff and students harmed by disempowerment, but the administration's ability to navigate the terrain is harmed also. Rather than spending their energy helping to create good programs and inspiring themselves and others to carry them out, administrators must spend a considerable portion of it controlling the actions of the powerless, who, of course, wish to gain power. A group that perceives itself to be lacking in power has but one fundamental interest:

to correct the lack of balance by acquiring power. Another negative result of the attempt to operate schools in linear, power terms is that concentrating the bulk of the power into one section tends to build layers of bureaucracy, an act which harms communication and makes decision making difficult.

Bureaucracy estranges faculty, students and lower levels of administration by speaking to them in policies and rules; it makes procedures more important than people. The bureaucratic emphasis is all wrong.

Wrong as it may be, however, a bureaucratic emphasis is common. Here is Hal McAninch, former president of the College of Dupage, Illinois, and former Acting Chancellor of the Community Colleges of Baltimore County in Maryland:

> On one hand, it is important that I try to be extremely open with faculty and available to them.... At the same time I recognize that you have to be clear regarding faculty involvement in the decision-making process. On the other hand, you don't want to create a situation which inadvertently allows follower expectation levels to be something you can't live with down the road. To give people the impression that they are making the final decision is wrong. (quoted in Rouche, Baker III and Rose, p. 257)

Indeed, the standard vocabulary in Rouche, Baker III and Rose's book is "leaders" and "followers." To divide people that way groups power in the leader's fist. Perhaps he will permit his subordinates to lobby for an action. Perhaps he will exercise power benevolently, for the good of everyone concerned. However he chooses to use it, though, he will protect his power by not allowing his "followers" to ever believe that they can make the final decision. Therefore, when the school plans and programs are discussed, it is never a question of what *we* will do. The question is always in the singular: what *I* will do.

The linear model divides people into leaders and followers. Leaders lead by reserving power to themselves. Perhaps this model is efficient, but when it operates, nothing gets transformed.

Transformation and Empowerment. Many faculty members and students have radically different ideas of what administrative leadership means and how administrators should conduct themselves. Said one professor of psychology, "The proper function of the administration is to provide me with the tools I need to do my job. The administration is there to serve me so that I can serve my students." A member of the student government association at his college agreed, while putting a slightly different emphasis on the situation:

> I'm the one who counts here, me and the other students. This college is supposed to be in business to educate me. It's function is to help me reach my goals by teaching me what I need to know to reach them. The faculty, the administration, the counselors - all of those people are only here because of me and the others. The goal of the president and the deans is not their own convenience, but my education.

The young lady quoted above has a firm grip on her own personal power. She does not, however, recognize that in order to her to reach her goals maximally and efficiently, a unity is required, a full team operating for a common goal. She still sees the situation in competitive terms. The new transformational model of leadership will work to protect her power while also serving to empower all of the parties on the campus, so that all will work toward the goal: excellence in all aspects of the operations of the college.

Bennis and Nanus (1985) emphasize the empowering function of transformational leadership when they conceptualize the leader as a social architect, an individual who "understands the organization and shapes the way it works." (p. 110) The social architecture the leader helps create, the authors say, "is an intangible, but it governs the way people act, the values and norms that are subtly transmitted to groups and individuals, and the construct of binding and bonding within a company." (pp. 110-111) People are moved to act not because of fear or the anticipation of an impending reward, but because they also bind and bond; they come to share the vision, rather than being compelled to execute it. They operate in their own interests because they feel that the institutions' interests *are* their own. There is no dichotomy between what they want for their students and themselves and what the school wants for them. Students feel no dichotomy between what they want and what the system wants; they feel they *are* the system. In this type of situation, all parties retain their personal power.

Under a traditional linear model, all of the disempowered groups are continually reminded that they do not have the authority to make a final decision. Each day they have their power diminished. Their loyalties are divided. The 1984 study of colleges conducted by the Carnegie Foundation for the Advancement of Teaching reported that professors no longer felt loyalty to their colleges. Instead they were loyal to their disciplines. It also reported that the administration of colleges is in crisis. Those two facts are directly connected; professors are disempowered by their schools but empowered by their disciplines. Their loyalty, therefore, goes to their source of power. That sort of division is ended with a systemic vision, which creates the binding and bonding that unites people, rather than the hierarchical division that divides.

Three Types of Social Organizations. Most writers on leadership describe three types of social organizations: the personalistic, the formalistic, and the collegial.

Personalistic. Probably the oldest, most discredited, but still the most pervasive category of leadership is the personalistic, which is characterized by the concept of the "charismatic leader." This category assumes that the qualities which create good leadership do not originate in the institution or the interaction of several personalities, but instead are imbedded like blood cells within certain people, who because of their unique personal qualities emerge as leaders.

Under this form, leadership is assumed to be a quality associated with the leader's personal attraction and appeal, his *charisma.* Therefore, leadership is not something that is done, it is something that one *is.* It is embodied within the person. The cliche "leaders are born, not made" is a statement of the personalistic philosophy.

Early research into the field of management and leadership tended to concentrate on what became known as a "great person" approach. It assumed that leadership was the result of a charismatic personality, that management was the corporate equivalent of Moses leading the people out of Egypt. A confusion between the person and the thing dominated the early research. Investigators felt that if they could identify the qualities or "traits" that the great leader embodied, then they could locate the key to effective leadership. Studies attempted to measure physical, mental, personality and emotional traits. Since the researchers assumed that all actions originated at the top and flowed down, the interaction between the leader and other people, or the leader and the situation, was overlooked.

As a result of this early research, great lists of traits appeared in the research, leading to an assumption that if a person simply put these traits on like a topcoat before going to work in the morning, then he too could be a charismatic leader. Because the trait was no more the person than a hubcap is the car, personalistic theories did not enlighten the field. Regardless of the fact that it did not offer great insights into the nature of leadership, the trait theory dominated the management paradigm for decades. Though the literature no longer speaks widely of trait theory, it is still widely practiced.

It is true that some people are able to achieve great results in leadership as a result of their personal charisma. It is true that a person's personality is a major factor in his ability to inspire. It is also true, however, that charisma and personality operate in conjunction with the charisma and personalities of other people involved in the task. The Great Man theory failed because it could not explain interaction.

Formalistic. A formalistic structure is linear. Under this model, the top administrator, the CEO, governs. The president becomes the ultimate authority and governs by establishing rules, policies and procedures. He then rewards those who carry out those rules and policies while punishing those who violate the parameters. He strives to have the people "under him," the "followers," comply with his rules and attempts to make sure that they do not deviate from his direction. He is the strong father and the followers are his children. The structure of a formalistic group is hierarchal from the top down. Organization charts are taken seriously. A member of the administration who insists that the chain of command be followed is demonstrating the mindset of the formalistic structure.

Under formalistic structures, the leadership is often directive and authoritarian. Although strong autocratic direction has its benefits, it also has serious drawbacks. Lippett and White (1958), for example, found that groups headed by authoritarian leaders generally have higher productivity levels. On the other hand, they also have lower morale and less personal satisfaction. Since their efforts are noted by either external rewards or punishment, people working under authoritarian conditions work most productively when they are being watched. Their work is not their own; control is always in the hands of others. For that reason, formalistic structures quite often use the implied threat of the unseen watcher. On other occasions, the threat is not implied; Administrators who pay unannounced visits to instructors' classrooms buy into the formalistic model.

This type of structure derails innovation; formalism does not encourage risk taking. Policy and mode of operation is already determined and arrives in the hands of an "underling" fully formed and already fleshed out; the person in charge of executing the policy does not add anything to it or make any changes in it. He is there to do, not think and often even the method he is to use is lined out. The thick curriculum guides handed out to elementary teachers in which every step of the lesson they are to deliver is explicitly stated is an example of operations under a formalistic structure. The adjunct previously mentioned who, upon receiving a model syllabus, assumed that she must follow it rigidly thought that she was supposed to operate under a formalistic model.

Since the authoritarian structure of formalism is centered in a complex system of top down rewards and punishments, which are codified in the written policies and rules, the methods of operation are seen by managers as representing the ideal. This is the way things are done, the thinking goes, therefore this is the way that things *should* be done. Under formalism, then, the main task is to maintain the status quo. (It will be remembered that maintenance was the task of the fourth generation of the community colleges' history.)

The use of this method is still widespread. Despite the colleges' talk about collegiality, the research of the Carnegie Foundation indicates that most colleges and universities fall into the formalistic category. Most community colleges follow this model also.

Collegial. Quite naturally, the majority of teaching faculty dislike the formalistic structure and lobby for a collegial one. Under a collegial model, issues are discussed by all parties or their elected representatives until a consensus emerges. The consensus determines the decision. Rather than a top down model, rather than a reward and punishment form of control, a collegial structure creates an informal community in which each interested party is able to assume a share of power. The theory stats that ideas compete, instead of people. Each interested party is expected to advocate for his idea and, after free discussion, the best one will emerge somewhat altered for the better but successful. The free give and take of discussion will sink unworthy proposals. No individual has any more power than the degree of his ability to influence the direction of the group.

Under the collegial structure, people interact as equals; each person participates in the making of the decision, so that the ultimate decision belongs to all of them. Being responsible for the development of the idea, each person then feels responsible for carrying it out.

Under personalistic and formalist models, authority is imposed from without. The leaders propose, the followers dispose. Followers, therefore, are tools for achieving administrative ends. The home office sets the sales goals, the buyers determine what will be sold, and the clerks stick it on the shelves and try to get it into the hands of the customers. Because they have no creative responsibilities, clerks are viewed as interchangeable and easily replaced.

In a collegial system, on the other hand, authority is self-imposed; involved people are in effect serving their own interests by serving the institution's interests. There is therefore little need to exercise authority over them; empowered and involved people rarely need the threat of an unseen watcher; they are valued for their individuality, as well as their individual contributions to the overall operation.

A president operating under a collegial system is simply one center of influence among many. Just as the other members of the governance structure are, she is expected to present ideas, lobby for them, and try to win consensus approval. She is also expected, however, to serve as an example of the group's aspirations. She does not so much demand as much as she models.

Does this mean that the president represents only the thinking of the faculty, staff and students, that she does not initiate, introduce and advocate for programs, procedures and issues? Not at all. Under a collegial system, she is expected to. She does not, however, insist on her way or the highway. Miller (1974) says that under a collegial system the president is responsible for defining and articulating the common good.

For this reason, the essential qualities of a collegial leader are soft ones: modesty, the ability and the willingness to listen to others, the ability to place the needs of others ahead of one's own, and the willingness to influence rather than command.

David Ponitz, president of Sinclair Community College, in Ohio describes collegial leadership in this way:

> Nobody has got a lock on truth. We talk about ideas, and after agreeing upon the parameters appropriate to the situation, we set about to reach a hybrid solution to the tough problems. Once we find the hybrid solution that fits the particular parameters, the individuals responsible for implementation are empowered with getting the task done. Not only has this approach worked, but it has proven to be a good training ground for those aspiring to higher levels of leadership.

The need for a new model of leadership. What is striking about these three theories - along with most of the others discussed in the journals - is that they originated in the corporate world, not in higher education. Colleges have tried to manage their activities by adopting and adapting theories designed for businesses and corporations. The result has been the confusion and disillusionment described by the Carnegie Foundation. The models have not worked for a simple but frequently overlooked reason:

colleges and universities are not corporations. Regardless of the fact that both educational and commercial institutions have bureaucratic charts tracing the levels of management, they are completely different systems. A corporation exists to sell a tangible product; Wal-Mart with nothing on the shelves is out of business. A school, on the other hand, deals in intangibles - education, learning, and thinking skills cannot be shelved. A customer goes to Wal-Mart to pick up something external to him. He goes to college, however, to release something that is internal. The product from Wal-Mart is already manifested in the world; the "product" from the community college is not. Trying to operate a college as though it were a commercial firm, therefore, is similar to trying to make a cat become a dog. It simply cannot work.

What is needed is a form of leadership that originates in and suits the schools. It is far beyond the scope of this book to attempt to build such a leadership model but we can at least discuss some of the qualities that would result from such a model. The remainder of this chapter will briefly highlight ten points which must be prominent in any model that will take the community colleges into the twenty-first century.

The new model of leadership would:

Recognize that the community college is a system. It would look at the institution systemically, instead of in a linear fashion. The community college is a creature that is more than the sum of its parts; it is a result of the interaction of the sum, an entity that comes into being in relationship. Most community colleges, however, continue to operate as though we were still in the age of the specialization. They divide and classify and attempt to impose a specialist vision onto the various parties; students study, professors profess, administrators administer. None, according to the way most schools operate, have anything to offer outside of their assigned role. If the school wants to be viewed as up to date, it claims that its professors are facilitators.

In the community college system, people from radically different backgrounds all come together to create a new whole. All influence the totality and, as a result, it is both a reflection and a creation of the influences. In an early study of Universities, specifically the University of Massachusetts, Reisman and Jencks (1962) determined that the students were all the same type of person. Most were from their home state of Massachusetts, all were intelligent, most were from families who could not afford the more prestigious private institutions. The researchers concluded that the high degree of homogeneity had a deadening effect on the university. The deadening effect, then, would be the result of a deliberately manufactured and enforced linear perspective.

The community college does not suffer from this type of forced homogeneity. It is nothing if not diverse. The diversity, which was built into its creation and was therefore present from the beginning, means that students have a wide variety of life experiences to contribute to the system; they very definitely contribute those experiences and therefore are always venturing outside of their assigned role.

The college is obviously a systemic whole. It is made up of *relationships* between the various parties; the parts are not actually separate and distinct but instead are intermingling; they are water from several glasses flowing together in a pool. The schools, therefore, must be seen as systemic wholes with irreducible properties.

To attempt to lead by specialist techniques is to attempt to impose a linear structure on the college. To do so is to continue to make the mistakes of the past.

Recognize that the community college is a unique institution.

The schools are not extensions of high schools. Neither are they simply the first two years of the university. They are *more* and they are *different*. As this book has maintained, the community college is something brand new in American higher education.

It is a particularly American institution that grows out of a very specific set of American myths. It has always reflected the spirit of our nation. The major myth that governed the rise of the community college is this: in this nation, anyone who can benefit from the process has both a right and an obligation to become educated. Higher education, then, should be the opposite of what the universities, based on the European models, had traditionally been; instead of *excluding*, they should *include*.

The community college is rooted in the American belief in the essential goodness, worth and ability of the common person. Where the universities educated the elite and reflected a belief that only the elite should be educated, the community college was the place of higher education for the rest of us. During the institution's rise, a major item in the critical debate raised by university scholars was the question of whether everyone could benefit from exposure to higher education. Community college professors recognized the irony early on and questioned what exactly was being implied by the phrases "benefit from" and "exposure to." Those phrases carry an implied judgment that reveals a belief in a conceptual difference between the common and the elite.

The history of American education is the story of a privilege for the upper classes being extended to the lower. Schools began for the children of the rich and spread to everyone else. College remained the province for the upper classes for the first century of American history. It took the establishment of the land grant colleges in the late nineteenth century to spread the idea of higher education. The community is to the twentieth century what the land grant college was to the nineteenth; it is the promise spread wide.

A community college that does not recognize its distinctiveness can only imitate; it cannot originate. To look to the high schools or to the colleges for a model is to declare that one's own experience is at best secondary. It is to value another way more than one's own, to pay constant tribute to one's own sense of inferiority. Community colleges are not inferior institutions. They are, however, *different* institutions. That difference should be cherished and it should be enhanced.

Currently, the community college suffers from an identity crisis. It has been so many things at once for so long that it is no longer sure what it is and therefore it cannot be clear as to what its goal and its mission is. Only new thinking from a new style of leadership will help resolve the identity crisis.

Restore the vision. Community college leadership has been problem-centered and pragmatic, with a close eye on day to day operations and little attention paid to the larger picture. As the number and type of programs spawned in response to perceived immediate needs, few administrators and thinkers were looking to the future. The schools resembled a corporation with its eye focused solely on the next quarter's balance sheet. As a result, the community college vision has been weakened to such an extent that few can actually say what the schools stand for at this time. The literature abounds with discussions of the confusion in direction. What caused the loss of certainty concerning the mission? What weakened the vision? Oddly enough, the very success of the community colleges has caused them to stumble, unsure and overly cautious, into a future in which their own fate is uncertain.

Originally, the vision was clear, precise and limited. The schools were designed to provide two years of post-high school education to qualified Americans; that was their mission and that was what they did. The success of that mission led to a broadening; the schools determined to widen access, to open up the doors to two years of higher education to virtually everyone. That task has also been accomplished.

Since the American myth says that there are many ways to reach every goal, all of the post-high school education the schools offered was not designed to lead directly into the universities. The schools led the way in providing training for people wanting to enter the corporations, the paraprofessional ranks, industry and the skilled trades. The schools accomplished all of this by reaction, though; their course was charted by forces outside of the system. As the schools learned to achieve a blend of academic and career programs, they discovered that the educational environment was taking an unanticipated tack. With the rise of the comprehensive community college, vocationalism became much more important and the balance was lost.

Vocationalism's carrying the day is not truly the problem. The problem is that the vision had been lost; no one could be quite sure where the day was carried. It is safe to say that most colleges today are operating by inertia. Few have mission statements and those statements which exist are so clouded in generalizations and abstractions that they do not actually guide. Few divisions or departments within the schools have mission statements. More important yet, few are certain of their missions.

The curriculum has become a sprawling, unfocused catalog of free elective options. For whatever reason, it has ceased to guide students, faculty or administration. Because it has fallen into the Hutchins trap of trying to be so many things to so many people, the college no longer tries to offer students a synthesis of the important branches of knowledge under a unified guiding idea.

As Brawer and Cohen (1996) say

> All curriculum is, at bottom, a statement a college makes about what it thinks is important. The free elective system is a philosophical statement quite as much as it is a curriculum based on the Great Books or one concerned solely with occupational education. It is an admission that the college no longer has the moral authority to insist on any combination of courses, that it no longer recognizes the validity of sequence or organized principles of curriculum organization. (p. 338)

Without a clear, coherent and consistent vision, an organization fails. Too much attention paid to this quarter's bottom line means that the future lurks just beyond the eyes' peripheral vision and edges ever closer. This is the situation the community college finds itself in as we enter the fifth generation of its history.

As part of the re-thinking of the curriculum, the community college should get out of the student salvaging business. Remedial and developmental programs eat up most of the colleges' budgets and return very little on the dollar. Dollars thrown into that arena are dollars tossed into a drying well. Very little water can be drawn from it and the cost can never be recovered. While it is true that the community colleges maintain an egalitarian stance, which declares that everyone who can benefit from it should have a shot at higher education, it is also true that the student has a responsibility to prepare himself for that shot. The colleges have stopped demanding that the students exercise their responsibility.

The student who can learn to read while succeeding at college level courses is an unusual individual indeed. Some states, such as Delaware, have recognized the folly of allowing people to take developmental and credit courses simultaneously and are now demanding that students successfully finish all developmental work before embarking on credit level programs. Other locations, in a mistaken notion of student-centeredness, insist that the student is entitled to proceed in whatever order he chooses. This situation is roughly akin to permitting a visitor to the zoo to enter whatever cage he chooses. The results are rarely pleasant.

It is not a student-centeredness act to push people onto a path that ends in failure. Nor is it an act of student-centeredness to encourage people into programs they cannot emerge from. To have a student's best interests at heart, one must demand that the student have his own best interests at heart and take steps to become responsible for his own learning. The student's success is his own responsibility, not the college's. To carry him plays into the cynicism that states that warm bodies in seats are all that the schools are interested in.

While it is desirable for colleges to get out of the student salvaging business, it may not be necessary for them to take that step. That role might be taken from them by the politicians who, throughout the country, are beginning to complain. Why should we pay for remedial work in college, they ask, then we've already paid for it in middle school and high school? How often are we supposed to foot this bill? These are legitimate questions which will have to be answered as the community college enters a new century.

Establish and respect boundaries. Previous incarnations of community college history have been characterized by sprawling, uncontrolled growth, by an outward flowing of the mission in ever expanding circles, as though a stone were tossed into a body of smooth water. This sprawl led to the weakening of curriculum. We have discussed the loss of sophomore courses, as well as the loss of entire academic programs, leading to the early transfer of many of the best and brightest students. The uncontrolled sprawl has also had other effects. As the mission expanded, the colleges' commitment to excellence suffered and the intellectual core of the schools began to melt down.

Consider that the general education curriculum is the core of the community colleges' efforts. This curriculum consists of those facts, ideas and values in our common culture that the college considers to be important enough to transmit to current generations. As a result of the sprawl, the general education curriculum is in danger. In fact, the sprawl has not only to a lessening of its importance, but also to a disagreement on just what general education is and should be. As early as 1977, for example, the Carnegie Foundation declared that general education was a disaster area. Tracing the origins of the disaster, Boyer and Levine (1980) identified three generations in the history of general education approaches in this country. The first was characterized by University of Chicago's great book curriculum - another contribution of Robert Hutchins - which started in 1928. The first generation's emphasis on the great books reflected a consensus on the goals and processes of general education programs. That consensus died in 1945. As society's needs widened, that year's Harvard Committee report on general education stated that specialized training must also be considered and that the crucial task of higher education was to find a balance between the transmission of the cultural heritage and the needs of specialized education. The operational definition of general education changed; more was allowed into the curriculum. The third generation of reform came to the community colleges from Miami-Dade Community College's 1975-1978 attempt to reform the field of general education. Miami-Dade felt their program was in crisis; no one quite knew what general education was or what should be included in the program. The result of Miami-Dade's efforts was a change in emphasis from what should be learned to the question of how to learn it. The curriculum was no longer based on the content, the stuff that should be learned, but on the process, the student's ability to learn in general. The result was an increase in the loss of focus.

New systemic boundaries are needed. Boundaries set limits. They indicate a place that will not be gone beyond, a demarcation point that will not be exceeded. Boundaries are a line drawn by a sword in the dirt. As far as schools go, boundaries are the educational equivalent of the business plan. They define both the direction and the limitations placed on possible products to handle. A plan, therefore, does not simply say what will be done; it declares what *will not* be done.

As stated previously, an open system is one that allows information to enter from many sources; it does not maintain the rigid boundaries that would close off or restrict input. Should the boundaries become so loose, however, that they no longer filter out *any* information, then they will become indistinct and the system will be threatened by the unfocused and uncontrolled influx of new sensory input. As the community college went from junior college to comprehensive community college, its boundaries were stretched almost to the snapping point. Without clear boundaries, a system seeks to exist.

Within the community colleges, many people fear boundaries, thinking they will cut off growth. They will not. Boundaries will, however, insure that the growth is morphogenic.

Clarifying the mission of the colleges would go a long way toward defining boundaries. Once the schools have decided which of their many efforts they wish to concentrate upon, then the act of releasing the rest will establish necessary boundaries.

Empower all elements of the faculty. Community colleges cannot continue to operate with three separate faculties. The lack of unity creates a tension that undercuts all of the healthy initiatives the schools undertake. A state of division causes trust to fade like summer dew. It also leads to people working at cross-purposes, emphasizing different goals, an action that will strain the systems' boundaries.

Consider the following hypothetical example. Wal-Mart's senior management determines a course of action and gathers input on the plan from the people down the line. Middle and junior management sign off on the plan and present it to the staff, who also indicate approval. All parties are agreed, then, that this plan constitutes the way to go. The plan is initiated and promptly dies because no one on any level of operation pays the least bit of attention to it; they all have their own plans or their own way of doing business and fully intend to continue doing things their way. Why did they, then, sign off on the plan? Because they've heard a thousand plans and don't trust any of them any more; they no longer even listen. Signing off is simply the easiest way to end the discussion that they don't want to participate in any longer.

The example sounds absurd, but it is common. Both Wal-Mart in the days following Sam Walton's death and Apple Computers suffered from this scenario. In higher education, though, this example is even more widespread. A version of it can be found on almost every campus.

Already, academic faculty and technical faculty distrust each other;

each is convinced that the other gets most of the pie, while it is forced to make do with flakes of crust. As stated earlier, though, the group most affected by the negative aspects of division is adjunct faculty. Since part-time faculty is ignored and treated as though it were the illegitimate stepchild of the colleges, adjuncts trust neither group. Nor do they trust the administration that adjuncts know is cynically exploiting them and does not have their best interests at heart. Full-time academic and technical faculty often distrust administration also because each group tends to view the administration as protecting the other group's interests.

For these reasons and because of the further reason that each group is convinced that it knows best what should go on in its classrooms, faculty very often will ignore an initiative that it has approved. Once trust is thrown into question, loyalties shift; protecting of perceived self-interest becomes pervasive.

Other problems accompany the loss of trust. It has been shown that the conditions under which faculty work lead to learned helplessness. To restore faculty trust, administrators will have to remove learned helplessness from the faculty groups and to restore the levels of commitment to the schools. The factor of commitment is even more immediate with adjuncts. As the situation now stands, adjuncts are quite naturally committed primarily to their own interests; they need full time jobs and will by necessity abandon their current school if one is offered. Full time academic faculty is, like the university faculty, more loyal to their discipline than to the institution, whereas vocational faculty identify most strongly with their occupational fields.

This lack of trust, commitment and identification results from the ways the community college administrators have operated in the past. The old linear thinking created these problems. The new systemic thinking will have to solve them.

Empower students. The most frequent faculty complaint is that the academic level of their students is simply too low. As far back as 1977, when faculty was asked "What would it take to make yours a better course?," over 50% answered, "Students better prepared to handle course requirements." (Brawer and Friedlander, p. 32)

The quality of students determines almost everything about the college. The academic level of courses has to be determined by the academic level of the people who will be taking them. What courses are offered is determined by the number of students likely to register for them, an indicator in itself of student ability and willingness. Every program in every school is affected by the nature of the students.

The level of students is currently viewed as low. In fact, most commentary on the community college, from the beginning until the present time, takes as *a priori* the low ability of the students. A level of truth exists in the assumption, of course; after all, fifty percent of community college students are in remedial courses.

It is also true that students become what they are assumed to be. In 1968, Robert Rosenthal and Lenore Jacobson published *Pygmalion in the Classroom*. Instantly popular with educators, this book introduced the concept of the self-fulfilling prophecy. The study reported on an experiment in which the authors provided teachers with false information about the students they would teach during the next academic year. The information provided indicated that the students could be expected to make significant academic gains during the coming year. Since the teachers expected improvement and treated the students accordingly, the children improved. Since then the notion of teacher expectations has been widely studied. Several decades worth of studies now indicate that the effects of teacher expectations on students are real. Studies in the self-fulfilling prophecy, therefore, demonstrate the learning power of expectations and teacher treatment. The studies indicate that students tend to become the people they are treated as; treat them as learners, they become learners. Treat them as people of limited ability, on the other hand, and they demonstrate limitations. To a great extent, students will deliver the level of ability that is expected.

Community college students are widely viewed as having lower levels of ability. Like carelessly poured champagne, the literature overflows with discussions of the difficulty of teaching them. Yet the literature also suggests that these students can be successfully taught. A strong body of ERIC literature demonstrates that students in developmental classes do emerge from these classes having achieved their goals.

The body of clinical work gathered by ERIC shows that when a comprehensive program that (a) pays attention to students, (b) offers forms of counseling along with instruction, and (c) demands results from students is offered, learning occurs. In other words, when teachers expect success and construct new programs that make it possible, even students of "lower ability" are able to profit.

The classification of lower ability then refers only to previous performance, not to ability. It describes the perceptions of teachers, administrators and scholars.

The community college prides itself on its student-centeredness. Yet it also rates its students as lower ability and weakens the curriculum to demand very little of them on the assumption that they are able to accomplish very little. This creates a self-fulfilling prophecy of a different sort: creating an expectation of failure, the colleges are rewarded with failure on the parts of their students.

As we have seen, expecting and demanding little does not empower students. Instead it removes their personal power. To empower students, one must take them seriously. One must offer a curriculum that does not pander to immediate wishes or offer instant gratification. One must offer a curriculum that, rather than being designed to shuttle people into entry level jobs that will disappear in five years, will enable people to be able to exercise critical and creative thought, be able to experience and know both cognitive and affective lives and to have the flexibility to adapt to an environment characterized by rapid and unpredictable change.

If the community college is to truly be student-centered, it must offer the students what they need, rather than what they want. A college is not a TV network; it should not operate according to popularity ratings. As one student said

> In the hierarchy of importance in the community college system, it seems that the individual student is ranked absolute last. A good system should be built individual by individual, not by the bureaucrats that are currently running our particular system into the ground. I want knowledge, not memorization skills.

To operate from a superficial view of student centeredness that does not encourage students to stretch themselves violates respect. It certainly takes power away from students and does not equip them to be able to either create or face a future. From the time the community college quit talking about educating students and instead spoke of "salvaging" them, the college stopped exercising leadership in the area of student development.

As a student comments

> Yes, some students do come to the community college for job skills but most of the students I know are here for the inexpensive education that only a community college can supply. We *are* planning to continue our education beyond the Associates Degree level and we *do* want more from life than a few isolated skills. *Skills* can only take you so far, whereas *knowledge* can carry you forever.

In summary, then, to concentrate on the basic level, to aim for the lowest common denominator as though education were no more than a sit-com, does not empower students. To substitute skill training for learning does not, either. To empower students is to think of them - and help them come to think of themselves - as the best they are, to see the potential in them and work to actualize it.

Become an intellectual force. The community college has long been seen as less a home of intellectual activity than the universities. Its origins, remember, are located in the effort to get the less academically accomplished students out of the universities. For too long, the schools have allowed other people's perceptions to shape their own perceptions of themselves; they have come to believe that they are of lower caliber intellectually.

The rise of the idea of comprehensiveness lowered the intellectual level of the schools even more dramatically. A school, for example, that equates Art History with Auto Mechanics, saying that as far as credits and diploma requirements go, each is the same, has lost its claim to intellectual rigor.

A school that views its students as not being equipped for college work can speak of excellence in press releases but cannot actually achieve it. Scholars of community colleges have routinely painted a portrait of a student body that cannot achieve. As we have seen, Dale Parnell bases the program he outlines in book, *The Neglected Majority*, on the premise that three out of four of our public school students will not achieve a baccalaureate degree. *"The great debate about excellence in education,* he writes, *"is closer to a monologue of the one-sided opinions of well-meaning individuals and groups who have little contact with non-baccalaureate-degree America.* (p. 6, emphasis in original) Parnell assumes that because the students will not, they cannot - a faulty assumption. He then builds a program which settles for less than the best based upon his own assumptions.

Patricia Cross agrees with Parnell and is quoted at length by him to bolster his argument:

> In the final analysis, the task of the excellent teacher is to stimulate "apparently ordinary" people to unusual effort. What do the reports on school reform have to contribute to that goal? In the first place, there is surprisingly little attention given to "ordinary people" in the school reform reports. There is the clear implication that the rising tide of mediocrity is made up of embarrassing number of ordinary people.... There is not a lot said in the education reports about how to stimulate unusual effort on the part of ordinary people that we seem to be faced with in the schools and in most colleges.... The tough problem is not in identifying winners; it is in making

winners out of ordinary people. This is, after all, the overwhelming purpose of education. (Cross, 1984, quoted in Parnell)

Parnell declares that his purpose is to make winners out of ordinary people; his way of doing so, however, is to redefine excellence and track the so-called ordinary people away from baccalaureate programs. Right now, the vocational pull of the community college is strong and in many cases mandated from the state or county governance system. In Maryland, for example, the Maryland State Board for Community Colleges' statewide master plan for 1978 to 1987 stated that the "increasing emphasis on occupational programs reflects changing values and attitudes among students and their families as to the level of education required to qualify for desirable employment opportunities. This shift is reflected in national projections predicting that throughout the next decade, 80 percent of available jobs will require less than the bachelor's degree" (1977, p. 34)

What will these jobs be? The U.S. Department of Labor reported that the major job openings are for "retail salesclerks, cashiers, stock handlers and similar jobs for which a bachelor's degree is not required." (Kuttner, 1983, p. 209) What this means is that the state has mandated that its community colleges train people for jobs for which no training is required.

One student discussed this trend in terms of the pre-professional technological programs that were overwhelming her campus:

> In my opinion, the goal of any good community college should not be to produce technological dummies who possess nothing but a skill. That's what trade schools are for. A college educated person should be educated in many aspects of the world around her, not just what she does for a living. We must not forget the importance of real knowledge, the kind of knowledge that cannot be obtained by the regurgitation of terms, but through the practice of critical thinking, analysis and reading.
> The fact that community colleges are pushing for a technologically advanced but humanities-void curriculum scares me. As a future educator and parent I fear that the 'progress' of the community college represents the progress of the world. In twenty years, will it no longer be important to be able to think for oneself?

A school that prepares its students to settle for such jobs as salesclerks, cashiers and stock handlers is not aspiring to excellence, either for itself or its students. It is time to once again think of "ordinary people" as being capable of excellence in all areas. Cross is right; the difficulty is in making them winners. Adopting an anti-intellectual stance and demanding very little of them is not going to make them winners.

Perhaps the key concept we should keep in mind is that, as the students' comments indicate, students continue to take the word college in the title of the institution seriously. Administrators, politicians, planners, faculty members and other movers and shakers should also.

Think long-term, instead of concentrating on immediate benefits. One problem with a technical-vocational focus is that such an orientation creates a focus on the immediate. Schools equating education with employment opportunities overlook the long-term needs of students, as well as their own long-term good.

Students aspire to be more than retail clerks or stock handlers. Indeed, these are the minimum wage jobs they already have; they use them to support themselves while attending classes. The goal for going to college is to be able to leave these jobs behind. They want more; they are devoted to the long-term view.

A 1992 study by the Center for the Study of Community Colleges looked into the type of program that they termed non-liberal arts and discovered that eighty percent of students enrolled in non-liberal arts courses could be found in four areas: Business and Office, Personal Skills and Avocational Courses, Technical Education and Trade and Industry. It is instructional to examine what offerings these categories contain. Under Business and Office can be found such programs of study as accounting, taxes, business and management, which are traditionally transfer programs since to practice in these areas generally requires a B.A. Also to be found, however, are such areas of study as paralegal preparation and airline ticketing and reservations, which do not require bachelor's degrees. The Personal Skills category contains slightly more than eighty percent of the for-credit non-liberal arts students. These people are taking physical education, orientation, or introduction to the library courses, which are often required of all students and lead to transfer programs. Career and life planning and other self-appraisal courses fall under this category.

Under technical education can be found computer offerings and communications technologies, including journalism, TV, newspaper reporting, radio announcing, photo journalism and other mass media courses. Fire, police and law enforcement technologies also fall into this category. Finally, under the umbrella term Trade and Industry can be found such offerings as the construction, automotive and aviation trades, as well as surveying, drafting, welding and precision metal work. The trade and industry category registers 18.6% of enrolled students.

What these figures indicate is that, even in non-liberal arts programs, the vast majority of students are enrolled in areas which lead to a B.A. degree. To think of liberal arts students as transfer candidates and non-liberal arts students as terminal is an error.

If that is the case, however, we have to ask why more students do not transfer. The answer is that they do, but not immediately. Because of the other obligations that non-traditional students are forced to handle concurrently, the average community college graduate takes five years to finish a two-year course of study. Nationally, some twenty-seven percent of those people transfer immediately to a four year institution. As the period of time between graduation from the two-year college lengthens, a much higher percentage transfers. (It is impossible to find an exact percentage of long-term transfers because statistics are not tracked after four years. The community college graduate is a potential transfer student for much longer a period of time than that.) The fact is that over the long run, after stopping-out, working for a period of time and raising children, students do transfer. They simply do so and work on their upper division courses at the same rate of speed they pursued their associate's degree.

To describe students as either transfer or terminal, then, is unrealistic. They are most often both. The students this CSCC study describes are not settling for a short-term benefit. These students' eyes are locked on the long-term prize. A school that aspires to excellence will also be fixed on that prize.

To serve these students, we must recognize the difference between training and education. To train a person is to help him develop specific skills in order to perform a specific function, to instruct a person in the proper methods for handling a welding torch, for example. Training is action-oriented. The way to evaluate training is to see if the person can perform the function; if he can, it has been successful. Training, therefore, is short-term and limited.

Education, on the other hand, enables a person to develop far more generalized and abstract skills. It aims to teach a person to think and feel, to achieve the intellectual flexibility to be able to handle whatever situation arises. In this way, education is not job- or situation-specific. Nor is it particularly oriented towards action. The way to evaluate education is to follow a person through his life and determine if he is able to cope with the changes that will inevitably come. Education, therefore, is long-term and unlimited.

The community college should have education, rather than training, as its goal.

Bring the bureaucracy under control. The systemic community college that the fifth generation of history requires will not be managed. It will be *led*. Its leadership will not be heavily bureaucratized because maintenance is not the goal. The status quo needs to be altered and managers cannot alter; they can only keep alive the past. The task now is to march into the future.

A bureaucratic model cannot lead the way to the future. Under a bureaucratic model, the president is the center of power and is responsible for the welfare and outcomes of the institution (Kerr and Gade, 1986). Centering power in the hands of a single "leader," the president, creates a model that suffers from two major maladies: it tends to perceive reality selectively and it communicates from the top down.

The selective perception of reality is noted in Birnbaum's research, which shows that under this model, presidents tend to perceive themselves as more effective than average and considerably more effective than their predecessors. They also claim that under their leadership, major improvements have been made on campus. They make these claims regardless of whether more objective evidence bears them out. (1986)

Top down communication tends to center power at the top of an organization chart; how much influence, autonomy and ability to act one has depends on his place in the chart: the closer to the bottom, the less his ability to exercise professional power. Since faculty and students are generally at the bottom of the chart, the people whose behavior has the largest amount of consequences have the least amount of influence.

A quick reading of the literature of college management and leadership reveals that the models have all been borrowed from the corporations. The fundamental flaw here is that corporations have a built-in test of their effectiveness: profitability. The community college lacks that test. Deegan (O'Banion, 1991) has pointed out that since community colleges, as service organizations, do not have profitability as an indicator of success, they tend to substitute growth and size. New students, new buildings, new programs demonstrate that they are succeeding. This measure makes it difficult for them to innovate.

> Every service institution likes to get bigger and, in the absence of a profit test, size and growth become the criteria of success. Stopping what has 'always been done' and doing something else are both difficult for these kinds of institutions. (209)

What has always been done is to increase the size of administration. A top down, bureaucratic model of administration, based on corporate models, has been the type that has been increased. When presidents begin referring to themselves as CEO's, a common corporate term which is becoming much more common in the community colleges, then something has gone wrong in collegiate governance. Community college educators have not developed original approaches to administration, having been content instead to try to run brand new institutions by methods developed for other purposes.

The community college is not a corporation. It does not, like Wal-Mart, import, stock and sell products; nor does it answer to stockholders each quarter. The Wal-Mart comparison is no more than a metaphor. To attempt to make it real is to do the college a disservice. To attempt to operate the community college as though it were a retail outlet is to devalue and disempower both education and the people who need to be educated.

Transform the institution by practicing organizational development.
When schools are in trouble, the administrators generally assume it is the fault of the staff. They therefore redouble staff development efforts, while failing to recognize that if the staff is not delivering, then their shortcomings are a symptom of a larger, systemic problem. The problem is generally within the organization as a whole, not any single aspect of it.

Therefore, the answer lies in organizational development, rather than staff development. What exactly is organizational development? In 1980, Fullan, Miles and Taylor combed through dozens of definitions in order to write one that encompassed the features of all of the major definitions of organizational development:

> Organizational development (OD) in school districts is a coherent, systematically planned, sustained effort at system self-study and improvement, focusing explicitly on change in formal and informal procedures, processes, norms or structures, and using the concepts of behavioral science. The goals of OD are to improve organizational functioning and performance. OD in schools has a direct focus on educational issues. (p. 135)

Since organizational development examines both formal and informal procedures, processes, norms and structures, a well-designed study can penetrate the bureaucratic myths and get at the ways in which the system actually carries out its operations. It is axiomatic of organizational development that a large difference can exist between the way a unit is *supposed* to operate and the way it *actually* does. By examining the possible dichotomies in organizational operations, it can determine the systemic truth of an organization.

Only when the systemic truth is discovered can true transformation occur. Schmuck and Runkel (1985) list six reasons why this is true:

One: Groups differ from a sum of individuals. A group takes on a systemic identity that is more than and different from the identity of the individuals which comprise the group. In order to function, an organization requires individuals to work together. Working together requires skills that cannot come from a single individual. Therefore, say the authors, "a school's potentiality is greater than the sum, but its performance might be less." (p. 6)

Two: Change occurs through subsystems. The notion that the work of a school comes from people cooperating means that change can only come about by directing the effort to the intact groups, the *subsystems*, rather than to individuals. For a dean to direct a division chair to bring about change will be self-defeating if the chair cannot identify and communicate with the right combination of subsystems. Inside a subsystem will be located the agents of change, the people who can get the job done. If the chair cannot locate and motivate these agents, change will not happen.

Three: Members' goals and motives have relevance. The actions of individuals are reflections of their personal and professional goals, as well as their social motives. People do not act in a vacuum. Unless deprived of free choice through an agency such as incarceration or the military, people do not act because they have been given an order. Behavior is the result of personal analysis and a personal decision; a person decides to act because she perceives that doing so is in her interests. Should a desired action fail that perceptual test, it will be carried out.

To redirect the actions of involved subsystems, such as professors, adjunct faculty, students or counseling staff, then, agents of change must know the members' goals and motives. If the desired change cannot be connected to those goals and motives, then the desired change will not take place. A common thread in the interviews conducted for this book was how hard it was to get people to follow through on actions that were requested of them. The difficulty originates in the fact that the actions were perceived as the administration's, not the individual's. To fail to carry out that wish is not an act of rebellion; the individual believes she is behaving appropriately and may, in fact, believe she is engaging in the desired behavior.

Consider the fate of hundreds of curricular models drawn up by experts and other specialists. From the work of the Committee of One Hundred to the New Math and beyond, all have met with a degree of failure and many have never been put into practice? Why? Because classroom rejected them and either refused to use them or gave them a perfunctory try and declared that they would not work. Since adopting such a program is a blow to a teacher's professionalism and autonomy, she has no vested interest in taking it on. Since she does not "own" the program, why should she be committed to it?

To get people to behave in a transformational fashion, then, a leader must help them "own" the transformation.

Four: Members' feeling have relevance. Should a member of a system become either frustrated or gratified, that member will become emotionally involved in the overall system. This emotional involvement will affect behavior. Since desired change depends on "knowing what actions people are likely to take, knowledge of others' feelings can aid coordination. Knowing members' feelings can be as useful to the school staff as knowing members' knowledge, skills, or other resources." (p. 6)

Five: Untapped resources have relevance. An old piece of conventional organizational development wisdom goes as follows: if you want to solve a problem, ask the people who are affected by the problem what should be done. The reasoning behind this bit of conventional wisdom is simple. Individuals and groups always have abilities, skills and wisdom beyond what is demanded of them. Even though they are unrecognized, these resources, often unused, exist and can be tapped in order to create desired change. What is needed to solve a problem, therefore, frequently already exists.

The hiring of a new administrator to guide the change is generally not necessary. It is, however, often the norm. It is also often a mistake. A person hired to guide change has no interest in solving the problem; he is much more interested in *managing* it. To solve the problem makes him redundant; it is therefore in his best interests to keep it alive. Again, his action does not constitute rebellion. He will feel that he is carrying out his mandate, but he will discover complexities within the problem that no one anticipated.

Six: Change comes from within. Although the decision to change is often imposed from without, the actual change comes always from within. The leader might desire the change, but it has to be created by associates, the people the literature inappropriately labels "followers." Every desired action must be sold. Wal-Mart knows that its customers do not care about a product until it is their's. Although they selected them, ordered them and paid for them, the management and staff do not think of the items on their shelves as their personal property. Instead, they are anxious to get rid of them and, if they cannot accomplish this goal quickly enough, they take further action, such as cutting the price. One major reason many service industries, such as community colleges, have such trouble innovating is that the leaders do not recognize the ownership principle; they tend to hold on to their plans and ideas, refusing to sell them or give them away to the people who actually have to use them. Many of the previously mentioned educational innovations, for example, failed because the scholars and experts who drew them up did not trust the classroom teachers who would have to actually use the programs; instead of involving the front line people, they tried to make the programs "teacher-proof." They could not give up ownership.

Recognizing the principle that ownership comes from within and that people can only carry out plans that they "own" can help create the energy and enthusiasm that transformational change requires. Failing to recognize the principle almost guarantees that change will not be successful.

Conclusion. To realize the community college's potential to transform itself into new and unique systemic institution that it already is in embryo, a new approach will be needed in the fifth generation. This book outlines one such approach. The argument behind this book is that failing to recognize its true nature led the community college to disperse its energy in a thousand directions; the schools failed to heed Robert Hutchins' early warning and tried to become something for everyone and thereby, as he warned, wound up satisfying no one. The schools took the Wal-Mart metaphor too much to heart and forgot that they were not, in actuality, a discount chain.

The hope of the book is that by recognizing its systemic nature and devising plans and strategies in line with it, the community college can transform itself once more and become the vital and unique contribution to American higher education that it needs to be.

Bibliography

American Association of University Professors (1981). *Part-time faculty series.* Washington, D.C.: AAUP

Baker lll, G. A. (1994) *A handbook on the community college in America.* Westport, CT: Greenwood

Baldridge, J. V. (1980) Managerial innovation. *Journal of Higher Education.* 51, 117-34

Bender, L. W. & Breuder, R. L. (1973) Part-time teachers: "Stepchildren of the community college. *Community College Review.* 1 29-37

Bender, L. W. & Hammons, J. O. (1972) Adjunct faculty: Forgotten and neglected. *The community and Junior College Journal.* 43 21-22

Bennis, W. & Nanus, B. (1985) *Leadership.* New York: Harper and Row

Biles, G. E. & Tuchman, H. P. (1986) *Part-time faculty personnel management policies.* New York: MacMillan

Blank, S. & Greenberg, B. (1081) Living at the bottom. *WPA: journal of the council of writing program administrators.* 5(1) 9-12

Blocker, C. E., Plummer, R. H. & Richardson, R. C. Jr. (1965) *The rwo-year college: A social synthesis.* Englewood Cliffs, NJ: Prentice-

Boyar, E. L. (1987) *College: The undergraduate experience in America.* New York: Harper and Row

Boyar, E. & Levine, A. (1980) *A quest for common learning.* Washington, D. C.: The Carnegie Foundation ofr the Advancement of Teaching.

Brawer, F. B. & Friedlander, J. (1980) *Science and social science in the two-year college.* Topical Paper # 71. Los Angeles: ERIC Clearinghouse for Junior Colleges

Brick, M. (1965) *Forum and focus for the junior college movement.* New York: Teachers College Press

Brick, M. & Karabel, J. (1993) *The diverted dream: Community colleges and the promise of educational opportunity in America.* New York: Oxford University Press

Brothers, E. Q. (1928) Present day practices and tendencies in the administration and organization of public junior colleges. *School Review.* 36, 665-674

Burns, J. M. (1978) *Leadership.* New York: Harper & Row

Cain, M. S. (1991) *Integrating adjunct faculty into a community college humanities division.* Ann Arbor: UMI Dissertation Information Service

Cohen, A. (1971) *A constant variable.* San Francisico: Jossey-Bass

Cohen, A, M. & Brawer, F. B. (1969) *Measuring faculty performance.* Los Angeles: ERIC

Cohen, A. M. & Brawer, F. B. (1987) *The collegiate function of community colleges: Fostering higher learning through curriculum and student transfer.* San Francisco: Jossey-Bass

Cohen, A. M. & Brawer, F. B. (1996) *The Amnerican community college.* San Francisco: Jossey-Bass

Cohen, M., March, J. & Olsan, J. (1974) A garbage can model of organizational choice. *Administrative Science Quarterly.* 17 1-25

Cooke, H. L. (1972) *Characteristics of part-time instructors in comprehensive community colleges of North Carolina.* Unpublished doctoral dissertation. Duke University

Cross, P. (1976) *Accent on learning.* San Francisco: Jossey-Bass

Deegan, W. L. (1989) Entrepreneurial management. In O'Banion, T. Ed. *Innovation in the community college,* New York:MacMillan

Deegan, W. L. & Tillery, D. (1985) *Renewing the american community college: Priorities and strategies for effective leadership.* San Francisco: Jossey-Bass

Deiner, T. (1986) *Growth of an American institution.* Westport, CT: Greenwood

Eaton, P. et al. (1992) *Probing the community college transfer function: Research on curriculum, degree completion and academic tasks.* National Center for Academ,ic Achievement & Transfer: American Council on Education

Eells, W. C. (1931) *The junior college.* Boston: Houghton-Mifflin

Fields, R. R. (1962) *The community college movement.* New York: MacMillan

Fox, G. C. (1984) Factors that motivate part-time faculty. *Community Services Catalyst.* 14(1) 17-21

Friedlander, J. (1979) Instructional practices of part-time versus full-time faculty in community colleges. Paper delivered at the Annual Meeting of the Association for the Study of Higher Education. Washington, D. C., April, 1979

Fullan, M. Miles, M. B. & Taylor, G. (1978) *OD in schools: The state of the art.* Toronto: Ontario Institute for Studies in Education

Gappa, J. M. (1984) Employing part-time faculty: Thoughtful

approaches to continuing problems. *AAHE Bulletin.* Ocyober, 1984 3-7

Garrison, R. H. (1967) *Junior college faculty: Issues and problems, a preliminary national appraisal.* Washington, D. C.: American Association of Junior Colleges.

Gleazer, E. J. (1980) *The community college: Values, vision and vitality.* Washington, D. C.: American Association of Community and Junior Colleges.

Goodman, P. (1964) *Compulsory miseducation.* New York: Horizon

Harper, R. W. (1903) The high school of the future. *The School Review.* 11 1-3

Harper, R. W. (1905) *The trend in higher education.* Chicago: University of Chicago Press

Kandzer, J. (1977) *A comparison of student ratings of teaching effectiveness for part-time versus full-time faculty in selected Florida community colleges.* Unpublished Doctoral Dissertation. Michigan State University

Kantroqitx, J. S. (1981) Paying your dues, part-time. In Desole, G. & Hoffman, L. Eds. *Rocking the boat: Academic women and academic processes.* New York: MLA

Keller, G. (1983) *Academic strategy: The management revolution in higher education.* Baltimore: Johns Hopkins University Press

Kennedy, G. (1967) Preparation, orientation, utilization & acceptance of part-time instructors. *Junior College Journal.* 37 14-15

Kerr, C. (1963) *The idea of the university.* Cambridge, MA: Harvard University Press

Laszlo, E. (1972) *The systems view of the world.* New York: George Braziller.

Leslie, D. W., Kellans, S. E. & Gunne, G. M. (1982) *part-time faculty in higher education.* New York: Praeger

Leslie, L. L. (1993) Acceptance of community college philosophy among faculty of two-year institutions. *Educational Administration Quarterly.* (9) 58-62

Lombardi, J. (1975) *Part-time faculty in community colleges.* Los Angeles: ERIC

Lorenzo, A. L. (1991) Anticipating our future purpose. *Community, Technical, and Junior College Journal.* 61(4) 42-45

orenzo, A. L. (1994) The mission and functions of the community college: An overview. In Baker lll, ed. *A handbook on the community college in America.* Westport, CT: Greenwood Press

McClelland, D. C. (1958) Methods of measuring human motivation. In Atkinson, J. W. Ed. *Motives in fantasy, action, society.* New York: Van Nostrand.

McGuire, P. (1984) Enhancing the effectiveness of part-time faculty. *Community College Review.* (3) *27-33*

Miller, D. J. & Ratcliff, J. L. (1986) Analysis of professional developmenmt activites of Iowa community college faculty. *Community/Junior College Quarterly.* 10-4 317-343

Morison, S. E. (1965) *The oxford history of the American people.* New York: Oxford University Press

O'Banion, T. (1972) *Teaching for tomorrow.* Tuscon: Universiy of Arizona Press.

O'Connell, T. E. (1968) *Community colleges: A president's view.* Urbana: University of Illinois Press

Palinchak, R. (1973) *The evolution of the community college.* Metuchen: The Scarecrow Press

Palmer, J. C., Ludwig, M. & Stapleton, L. (1984) *At what point do community college students transfer to baccalaureate-granting institutions? Evidence from a 13-state study.* Washington, D. C.: American Council on Education

Parnell, D. (1985) *The neglected majority.* Washington, D C.: The community College Press.

Pincus, F. L. & Archer, E. (1989) *Bridges to opportunity: Are community colleges meeting the needs of minority students?* New York: Academy for Educatrional Development and College Board.

Postman, N. (1979) *Teaching as a conserving activity.* New York: Delacorte

Probing the community college transfer function. (1994) Washingtin, D. C.: American Council on Education

Reisman, D. & Jencks, C. (1962) *The academic revolution.* New York: Doubleday.

Roberts, E. (1976) *College leadership for community renewal: Beyond community-based education.* Quoted in Witt, A. A. et al (1994) *America's community colleges: The first century.* Washington, D.C.: American Association of Community Colleges.

Rosenthal, R. & Jacobson, L. (1968) *Pygmalion in the classroom* New York: Oxford University Press

Rouche, J. E., Baker lll, G. A., & Rose, R. R. (1989) *Shared vision: transformational leadership in American community colleges.* Washington, D. C.: The Community College Press.

Schmuck, R. A. & Runkel, P. J. (1985) *The handbook of organization development in schools.* Palo Alto: Mayfield

Seidman, E. (1985) *In the words of the faculty: Perspectives on improving teaching and educational quality in community colleges.* San Francisco,: Josseyy-Bass

Seligman, M. (1975) *Learned helplessness.* New York: Harper and Row

Speer, C. (1970) Family ststems: Morphogenesis and morphostasis, or is morphostasis enough? *Family Process.* 9(3) 259-277

Steinbeck, J. (1941) *Log from the sea of Cortez.* New York: Viking Compass

Tuchman, H. P. (1981) Who is part0time in academe? *AAUP Bulletin.* 65 745-760

Waddell, T. K. (1978) *Part-time faculty in Arizona community colleges.* Unpublished doctoral dissertation. University of California

Wallace, M. E. (1984) *Part-time employment in the humanities.* New York: MLA

Watzlawick, P, Beavin, J. & Jackson, D. (1974) *Pragmatics of human communication.* New York: W.W. Norton

Yang, S. W. & Zak, M. W. (1981) *Part-time faculty employment in Ohio: A statewide study.* Kent, OH: Kent State University

Index

adjunct faculty, 44, 53-73, passim
American Association for Community and Junior Colleges, 31, 86
Apple Computers, 129

Baldridge, J. V., 99
Becvar, R. J. and Becvar, D. S., 19
Bender, L. W., 65
Bennett, R., 96
Bennis, W., 38, 98, 99, 104, 105, 115, 118
Bensimon, J., 79, 93, 105
Biles, G. E., 68, 70, 71
Birnbaum, N., 93, 105
Blocker, C. E., 102
boundaries, 34, 35
Boyar, E. 96, 98
Brawer, A. M. 49, 51, 81, 96, 126
Brick, M., 109
Brothers, E. Q., 99, 100
Burgess, J. W., 28
Burns, J. M. 105

Cagle, G. A., 66
career patterns, 72
Carnegie Foundation for the Advancement of Teaching, 63, 97, 98, 118, 122, 113, 114
Center for the Study of Community Colleges, 82, 135
charisma, 4
Chicago, University of, 5, 128
Clinton, President W. J., 1, 6,
Cohen, A. M. 7, 49, 51, 68, 79, 89, 93, 128
collegial model, 113
communication, 19-21,
Compton, D. G., 72
Council of Writing Program Administrators, 62

Cross, P., 87, 133, 134
curriculum, 12, 128-130

Deegan, W. L., 27, 28, 31, 36, 51, 103, 137
Diverted Dream, The, 1, 104
dropping out, 89-90

Eels, W. C. 7, 97
ERIC, 131

Fields, R., 45
Form, 74
formalistic organization, 112

Friedlander, J, 68, 69, 70, 71
Fullan, M., 138

generational history, 27-39
Golden Age of Administration, 91
Goodman, P., 8
Governance, 89-104, 121-133
Great Books Curriculum, 129
Great Person Approach, 111
Grieve, R., 66

Harper, W. R., 29, 30
Harvard Committee on Curriculum, 128
Homeostasis, 17
Hooker, J., 73
Hutchins, R., 7, 33, 128

Jacobsen, L., 131
Jencks, C., 123
Jiffy Lube, 16

Kandzer, J, 66, 67, 68
Kantrowitz, J. S., 71
Karabel, J., 93, 94-95
Keller, G., 93, 94-95, 100, 111
Kennedy, G., 67

Kerr, C., 94
Kraus, C., 68

Laszlo, E., 13, 14
leadership, 89-94, 121-123
learned helplessness, 73-75
Leslie, D. W., 47, 62, 104
linear and systemic models, 9-23
Lippitt, R., 112
Log From the Sea of Cortez, 14
Lombardi, J., 67
lower ability see students, lower ability
Ludwig, A., 90

management, see leadership
Maryland State Board for Community Colleges, 134
McAninich, H., 117
McClelland, D. C., 64, 65
McGuire, P., 70
Merton, R. K., 93
Messerschmidt, T. C., 65
Miami-Dade Community College, 128
Michigan, University of, 93
Miles, M. B., 138

Miller, D. J., 74, 122
Millet, G. A., 98
minority mentality, 70-71
mission, community college, 46
Modern Language Association Statement on Part-Time Faculty, 71
morphogenesis, 15, 18
morphostasis, 16
motivation see students, motivation of

Nanus, B. 39, 98, 99, 104, 105, 115-118
National Center for Educational Statistics, 62-63
Neglected Majority, The, 1, 108, 133
Neumann, E., 79, 100
Nitty-Gritty Dirt Band, 11, 12
Non-traditional students see students, non-traditional

Organization, social, 119-122
　collegial, 121
　formalistic, 120
　personalistic, 119
Organizational Development, 138-141

Parnell, D., 1, 108, 133, 134
patchwork governance, 97
political model, 99
Plummer, R. H., 102
Ponitz, D., 122
Postman, N., 18
power, 49-53, 73-75, 129-131
powerlessness, 49-53, 73-75, 129-131
President's Commission on Higher Education, 33, 34, 35, 103
Pygmalion in the Classroom, 131

Reisman, D., 123
Rosenthal, R., 13
Richardson, R. C., 102
Runkel, P. J., 123

Schmuck, R. A., 139
Seidman, E., 52
Seligman, M., 73, 75
self-fulfilling prophecy, 131
social organization see organization, social
specialization, 10-12
Speer, C., 15
Steinbeck, J., 14, 15
stopping out, 89-90
students
　changing definitions of, 82
　lower ability of, 87-89, 90-94
　motivations of, 80-82
　nontraditional, 80-82
　systemic interaction with community colleges, 85-87
　transfer, 88-90
Systems Theory, 9-26, passim

Tappan, H., 28
Trait theory, 111
transfer students see students, transfer
Truman, President H. T., Truman Commission, 33, 34, 35, 103
Tuchman, H. P., 62

U. S. Department of Labor, 134

vision, 115-116

Waddell, T. K., 68
Wallace,, M. E., 64, 71
Walton, Sam, 113, 129
Watzlawick, P., 20